THE QUIET CORNER

*Dedicated to my Son
in memory of
my Father*

The Quiet Corner

by

John S Matthew

compiled and edited
with additional material by

Stewart Matthew

THE SAINT ANDREW PRESS

EDINBURGH

First published in 1990 by
THE SAINT ANDREW PRESS
121 George Street, Edinburgh EH2 4YN

ISBN 0 7152 0645 1

British Library Cataloguing in Publication Data
Matthew, Stewart G
Quiet corner
1. Sons. Interpersonal relationships with fathers.
Christian viewpoints
I. Title
261.8358742

ISBN 0-7152-0645 1

Cover design by Mark Blackadder
Illustrations by Gillian Murray

This book has been set in 9.5/12 pt Helvetica
and 12/12pt Garamond
with Avant Garde

Printed and bound in Great Britain by Bell & Bain Ltd., Glasgow

*The Publisher acknowledges
financial assistance from
The Drummond Trust towards the
publication of this volume.*

CONTENTS

CONTENTS

◊

CONTENTS

◊

◊

ABOUT THE WRITERS

John S Matthew

BORN IN 1910. Little is known about his childhood. It was probably not very happy, although his relationship with his mother was a beautiful one. He loved her dearly.

His formal education ended at 14 years of age when he went to work to support his mother financially. Without success he tried to persuade her to leave her home and difficult husband. He worked as a journalist and briefly as a short story writer before the Second World War destroyed his writing career.

In 1938 he married Gladys Mortimer. Their son, and only child, Stewart, was born in November 1939.

Most of his working life after the war was as a salesman, first of sweeties until he graduated to paint brushes.

Life was never financially easy for him. His literary and journalistic skills found expression in his editorship of *The Wyvern*, the magazine of the congregation of which he was a member. He became an Elder in the Church of Scotland, looked after a district, pursued his understanding of the Bible, and became a much used Reader in the Church.

He was a complex man probably little understood; a man who deserved much more love and affirmation than he got.

ABOUT THE WRITERS

Stewart Matthew

As a young boy Stewart only survived one day in a Sunday school. He did however begin to go to Sunday worship with his parents. His father was the main influence in this direction.

As a teenager the call to the full-time Christian ministry began to shape his life. Thanks to one particular secondary school teacher he got out of school with enough qualifications to enter university. During his university days he acquired the degree of Master of Arts in Social Sciences, and the Bachelor of Divinity degree. Before leaving university he got married.

After university he completed his training for the parish ministry, but then went for a period to England to teach Religious Education in a large Comprehensive school in Yorkshire—his 'missionary period'!

While in England, his wife gave birth to their very first child—a daughter called Debbie.

He returned to Scotland to the parish ministry in Kilmarnock in 1969, and to the family was added a son—Stewart Andrew.

In 1979, just after the death of his father, Stewart joined the staff of the Church of Scotland's Department of Education.

Since 1988 he has been fighting a battle against a kind of cancer known as lymphoma. This book was compiled during that battle.

PREFACE

THE QUIET CORNERS on the following pages were written by my father between 1953 and 1979. They appeared first in *The Wyvern*, the congregational magazine edited by him for some seventeen of these years.

Recently I was kindly given, by the present minister of that congregation, the congregation of my childhood, my father's personal bound set of all the *Wyverns* he had edited.

My relationship with my father was not a particularly easy one, to the hurt of both of us. It was touching for me to read these magazines. They brought back memories of him and provided me with some more insights into his life.

In recent years I have had one or two books published. It has been a source of great sadness to me that my late father has not been able to share the excitement of publishing these books. No matter what anyone else feels or has said, he would have been proud of them, or at least of me; not that he would have necessarily said so. It would have been left to someone else to tell me, probably my mother had she been alive.

My father has recently been very much in my mind, and I have wanted to put some of his written words into print. I hope you enjoy what we together share with you in THE QUIET CORNER. My own contribution has been to select some of his QUIET CORNERS, and to add thoughts sparked off by them for me, along with some reflections on our relationship as father and son.

Stewart Matthew
March 1990

I said a prayer for you today
And know God must have heard;
I felt the answer in my heart
Although He spoke not a word.

I didn't ask for wealth or fame
(I knew you wouldn't mind);
I asked for priceless treasures rare
Of a more lasting kind.

I prayed that He'd be near to you
At the start of each new day,
To grant you health and blessings fair,
And friends to share your way.

I asked for happiness for you
In all things great and small,
But that you'd know His loving care
I prayed the most of all.

Anon

◊

Mother Love

MOTHER LOVE—is there a more remarkable phenomenon, or richer blessing, on the face of this drab, man-spoilt earth? I remember once on an island off the coast of Scotland, hurriedly pushing off in a boat to the rescue of a small boy in difficulties in the

bay. The cries of his friends attracted his young mother in her cottage nearby. One glance took in the scene. Fully clad she dived in and, cleaving the sea like a fish, she reached the drowning boy half a boat-length ahead of me. The boat was handy, but not actually needed. The boy was safe, quite safe—in his mother's arms.

Oddly enough, you know, that lass actually hadn't a good reputation as a mother. Her husband was at sea and many a black and blue mark she bore when, on his return, he learned that the three young children had again been left whole evenings to their own devices, whilst she went dancing with the officers at a distant camp. 'Some mither that,' they said in broad local patois, and they would spit contemptuously. Some mother—but when the time of testing came, she rose supreme to meet her bairn's need.

The tremendous power of mother love was never brought home to me more forcibly than the other day in Kirkcaldy when I had to take to hospital the little five-year old chap who had the misfortune to sever his right hand at the wrist in a butcher's shop. If I was frankly amazed at the courage of little Michael who, even at that tender age, showed that he was of the stuff that men are made of, I

2

was humble before the desperate courage of yet another young mother. Quite concealing her own pain and torment, she spoke quiet words of comfort and reassurance to her sorely afflicted bairn and clasped him warmly, protectingly to her breast.

January 1959

On page 5 you will find a poem which my father says his mother read to him when he was young. Perhaps she was the source of his life-long love of literature. His father would not have been a likely source. I met him when he was old, mellowed and dying; by then, my father told me, a very different man.

I never met my father's mother. She had, I think, died before I was born. I know she was greatly loved, even revered, by him. But I cannot remember him speaking about her to me. To have done so would perhaps have caused him much emotional pain. My own mother, who usually had to interpret to me what my father meant and felt about anything, especially about *me*, told me how much he had loved his mother. The next QUIET CORNER may owe its title to her.

My father left home as a boy, one reason being to escape his explosive father. He wanted his mother to go with him, but, I was told, she was the older type of Scottish wife who, no matter how many walls she was thrown against on drunken Saturday nights, did not leave her man.

Mothers appear in many of my father's QUIET CORNERS. They do so as loving people, although not flawless people.

Fathers, from my father, did not receive such good press!

A Mother in a Thousand

QUIET CORNER

'AS MEAN as sin! Even though she is a widow, she's no' as hard-up as a' that.' That was what the gossips said about Maggie Blair many years ago, and this is the story of how the gossips were wrong—as they almost invariably are.

Jamie Blair was a small lad and as he grew older it hurt him to realise the criticism of his mother that was implied in the tightness of lip, the shrugged shoulders of the neighbours. His mother, he knew, was far from well off, with two or three regular cleaning jobs, but on Friday evening, as she laid out every penny on the kitchen table, allocating what was needed for the barest necessities and putting the rest carefully aside to go to the bank next day, he sometimes felt in his own heart the tiniest twinge of disloyalty and doubt.

There was little or nothing for sweets that other lads had in plenty. His clothes were patched but adequate; his mother was downright shabby, even at church, to which she would have dragged herself with her last breath. A close woman they called his mother in his very hearing and he wondered, was it really necessary that every single penny should go into the bank book, which she also seemed to worship?

Curiously, the quiet dominie did not share the local viewpoint, and often as he gave up spare time to coach his most brilliant pupil for the academy bursary exam, he would say musingly and cryptically, 'Honour your mother, Jamie Blair. Some day you will realise she is a most remarkable woman'. At last the time came for the dominie to explain. Jamie was to go right through the academy and, thanks to the long years of skimping and scraping by his mother, there was, if he continued to work hard, the glittering prospect of a career at the University!

Let us skip the long story of Maggie Blair's continued struggle, of how young Jamie himself shivered and studied in cold digs by candlelight, how he wore his boots till they would no longer mend and how he often went to bed in the early hours with his healthy young appetite unabated.

At the end of it all, Jamie Blair emerged with his degree in divinity and, seeing in him the germ of future greatness, a famous preacher in a famous church in Edinburgh took him as his assistant.

The first time Jamie Blair preached from that famous pulpit, Maggie Blair was seated in an unobtrusive side pew to hear with humble pride what her son had to say.

Jamie Blair had learned much with the years. His sermon over, his duty to God and to the congregation done, he turned right round and he bowed low in gratitude to the shabby, tired little woman who, under God's grace he now knew, had been the real author and finisher of it all.

October 1963

4

Little Boy Blue

PLEASE—this has nothing to do with 'come blow your horn'!

It is the title of the tenderest children's poem I know, one my mother used to recite to me when I was a child. I rejoiced to come upon it 40 years later in the *Children's Encyclopaedia* under the by-line of Eugene Field. I took a copy, which I proceeded to mislay and have only re-found, 20 years further on! By re-publishing it in *The Wyvern* I feel it might be cut out by some and stored away and perhaps, in future years, continue to give pleasure to countless people.

The little toy dog is covered with dust,
But sturdy and staunch he stands:
The little toy soldier is red with rust
And his musket moulds in his hands.
Time was when the little toy dog was new,
And the soldier was passing fair.
And that was the time when Little Boy Blue
Kissed them and put them there.

Now, don't you go till I come,' he said,
'And don't you make any noise!'
So, toddling off to his trundle-bed,
He dreamt of the pretty toys.
And as he was dreaming, an Angel song
Awakened our Little Boy Blue.
Oh, the years are many, the years are long,
But the little toy friends are true!

Faithful to Little Boy Blue they stand,
    Each in the same old place,
Awaiting the touch of a little hand,
    The smile of a little face.
And they wonder, as waiting the long years through,
    In the dust of that little chair,
What has become of their Little Boy Blue
    Since he kissed them and put them there.

John Matthew, 1924

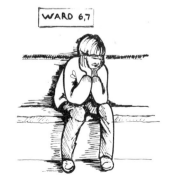

◊

The Little Chap Who Waited
*—and the Novelist whose heart was big enough
to bear sorrow greater than her own*

QUIET CORNER

IN THE BIG American hospital the Head Nurse spoke regretfully. 'Ah, Mrs Norris, you were to have adopted the Simmons' baby. I am very, very sorry . . . .'

So Kathleen Norris, premier American writer of fiction, received one of the big blows of her life. But the nurse would not let her dwell upon it.

'You think you've trouble on your hands. Listen!'

Had Mrs Norris noticed the shabby little fellow cooling his heels on the bench in the crowded corridor? No? He was the son of a French girl employed in a local laundry. They only had each other in the world, and while the young mother was fighting her losing battle against illness, the boy spent all his waking hours waiting out there till she should call him.

Tell him to go home? He and his mother had the corner of a slum —whilst she was able to iron and pay for it. Indeed he had no home where she was not.

Besides, the losing battle was over and now it was the nurse's task to tell a child of eight that there was no point in waiting there—no, not even as quietly as a mouse—since he was now alone in the world.

A wise woman the nurse, 'I don't suppose you would go out there and . . . tell him for me?'

We can imagine how Kathleen Norris, a kindly woman, went into the crowded, ether-smelling corridor to 'casually' meet the lonely little fellow

7

who kept faithful vigil. She was waiting too, and would like some lunch, if only she hadn't to go alone. Would he care to come too?

He was sorely tempted, but staunchly shook his head. He was to be called the moment his mother awoke. If she called and they couldn't find him, just what would she think?

It could all be arranged, Kathleen Norris explained. They would leave word at the lodge where they would be, and the nurse could telephone, if she should wake who would not wake again.

By the time they had their meal they were getting on famously and the same device lured him to her home. It was late that evening when a tired little chap learned the truth, but by then it was a friend who was telling him, and it was a friend in whose comforting arms he cried himself to sleep.

Kathleen Norris adopted the boy and he grew to adore and cherish her for the qualities of sweetness and compassion which had prompted her to help in the bearing of sorrow greater than her own.

'Of such is the Kingdom.'

January 1954

'You've Skelt my Cigarette Cards!'

QUIET CORNER

RECENTLY THE minister was speaking strongly about the virtue, indeed the necessity, of being a good neighbour. He had hardly time to get round to warning that if you try to put the theory into practice, you must be prepared for many a sore dunt! It was a bitterly cold night in Forfar a few years ago, snow everywhere, an icy blast that would have cropped your very ears off. I was heading for home when I noticed the High Street bus queue huddled miserably, waiting for transport. Poor souls, I thought. I can't do much, but what a pity to pass with an empty car when somebody might be catching pneumonia! I drew up at the Dundee stop. 'I've three empty seats,' I said, 'if anyone wants a lift to Dundee . . . .' The leaders of the queue, a lady and two men, stared at me stonily and in silence. I looked appealingly down the queue. 'Does anyone want a lift to Dundee?' Stoney stares; utter and complete silence. I stood for a moment in embarrassment before darting inside and driving off. Didn't they like the look of me? Impossible! Did they think I was after money?

You probably know the story of the man who flung himself into the canal, fully clothed, to save a lad from drowning. Drenched, his clothing ruined, he hurried home, to answer a knock later in the evening from a grim-faced woman. 'Was it you that took oor Wullie oot o' the canal?' Yes, it was. No light of gratitude softened the fond mother's eyes. 'What did ye dae wi' his bunnet?'

Only a story? It couldn't happen? At school years ago I yanked a day-dreaming youth out of the path of a careering tramcar. Gratitude as the tram, with screaming brakes, missed us both by inches? 'Look what you've done,' he exclaimed. 'You've skelt my cigarette cards!'

April 1964

Of Angels Unaware!

HAVE YOU ever entertained an angel unaware? In my case, I rather fancy it was an angel who entertained me!

She was my first landlady. A person less like the traditional angel than Kate Kirk it would be hard to imagine. She was small and plain and the care of an aged mother and the drinking habits of her feckless brother, apple—rotten—of his mother's eye, ensured that at all times she was pinched, shabby and deeply concerned with making ends meet.

'Poor Kate Kirk,' the ladies of her small town church called her. A devout attender, she was charitably permitted to toil in the background, but of course she could never be taken on a committee or anything like that. You couldn't introduce important guests, county people, to a self-effacing little woman who had only one coat, which had once been brown or bottle-green and was now with age a depressing mixture of both. 'Kate's coat of many colours.' Without resentment she overheard it so described by a lady who could ring

9

elegant changes upon three fur coats, paid for by a husband whose shady dealings were notorious.

As a young reporter in a county town, my dressing-table was at all times littered with uncherished tickets for concerts, talks and tea meetings. There was no need to attend such things when the necessary paragraph could easily be picked up later.

Those tickets fascinated Kate. To her they were pasteboard passports to Wonderland. She fingered them over and over again.

'Look here, do you want any of these things?' I asked her finally. 'Take a couple; help yourself to a handful.'

Kate shook her head sadly. There was her mother to look after —always mother—although she was well and wiry, long to survive poor Kate whose very months, it so happened, were sharply numbered.

There was no question of her brother staying at home from the pub to allow his sister out for one night; neither would his mother expect it. It was Kate's duty to stay; Kate's alone.

Yet hopes are dear, even the modest hopes vouchsafed to the disparaged Kates of this earth. Dwelling long and carefully over the selection, she at last chose her ticket. Surely to this one function she, a grown woman, might be permitted to go.

Normally I do not eavesdrop, but Kate's nervous delay in 'telling her mother,' her growing tension as the date approached, alerted me to the old woman's raised, querulous tone. I stopped in my tracks, realising that permission was not to be granted . . . .

Do not worry. Kate went to her concert. I might blush to recall the bluntness of speech which for the first time assailed the ears of a perfectly nice and merely spoilt and selfish old woman. Yes, when I had done, Kate went to her concert, and came back as though treading upon the stars.

If she could read this, I can practically hear her say—'What, my name in print? *Goodness me!*'

Kate never spoke two truer words.

January 1956

10

I have little or nothing by way of audio or visual aids to help me re-member my father. I discover that I know little or nothing about his childhood and teenage years. Sadly, I know very little about him at all at depth. We didn't talk enough at the feelings level.

His QUIET CORNERS seem to point to an upbringing and times spent as a journalist which gave him an eye for life's pathos—its rich-ness, pain, beauty and ugliness.

The recognition of not having shared enough at depth with my father, has made me try to share more with my children. I hope they will have more to remember me by than my array of neatly ordered photograph albums, and a stack of audio and video cassettes.

The Common Street

QUIET CORNER

THERE IS a vivid poem which describes a drab, dirty, depressing street. Evening comes, and the sun, slanting through the sullen clouds, streams down the grimy, rain-soaked street, transmuting it to gold.

I was reminded of that in an Angus mill recently, when I watched a girl at work. She was a plain lass, covered with the dust rising from the jute which she threw endlessly on to a rattling and thumping conveyor belt.

'Don't you get tired doing that?' I asked her.

She shook her head. 'Why no, I'm married you see, and the money I earn goes to furnish our room. We want it to be just right this summer.'

She stopped. Her cheeks were pink. She was no longer plain. No one is ever plain who even hints at secret, cherished, lovely things. She smiled, and the outcast sunshine seemed able to seep in through grimy panes, into that place where, before uncomprehending eyes, a drab and uninviting job was woven into dreams!

'*And, to the Common Street,*
A golden highway to a golden Heaven . . . .'

March 1954

◊

The Boy Nobody Cared For

QUIET CORNER

Billy had no father anyone could point to. Billy was tough, aggressive, always in trouble. He swore like a trooper. But who could look into those blue, hurt eyes—like those of a whipped puppy—and declare that Billy was not more sinned against than sinning?

HE MUST be nearly a man by now. If youthful proportions have fulfilled their promise, his stature alone should be sufficient to discourage all audible whispers about the father who did not stay around long enough to see what would become of Billy.

Billy's clothes were durable and merely dirty. He was not quite neglected, just unwanted. But with a feckless mother actually pretending to be his sister, and a tired old grannie whom he was taught to call his 'mam', was it any wonder there was sometimes in Billy's eyes the perplexed look of a whipped puppy?

If his eyes betrayed unhappiness, that was all the weakness that Billy would concede to a world which esteemed him good gossip  value and which overlooked—as did his own foolish mother—a small boy's natural wish to be loved and wanted. To an uncaring world, therefore, Billy presented if not a ragged, at least an unkempt aggressiveness. Feeling himself somehow inferior to other children, he normally reacted by bullying them unmercifully, and their respective mothers waxed wroth.

Billy swore like a trooper. Though clumsy in ordinary speech, Billy could swear with the ease and grace of a drill sergeant. Trouble was bound to ensue.

Billy was always on his best behaviour on Saturday afternoons. That was the afternoon when I generally brought a good broad-beamed boat round the coast to the little strip of sands, sweetly named the Bairns' Beach, and took all the youngsters in the district for a sail around the harbour. Naturally I welcomed all comers, but one Saturday I eyed the seraphically smiling Billy with dark disfavour as he came  ambling at the heels of the others. His swearing was becoming a minor scandal. He had even got the little girls started on the simpler words . . . .

It had to stop. I did not quite meet his eyes as I pronounced his sentence. 'Billy, I'm not taking you with me today. You've no right to swear the way you do. You've got little Sheila at it— and her just a baby. If things are different you can come next Saturday . . . .'

I can only imagine his unkempt, forlorn figure standing there alone as I resolutely pushed off from the shore.

Next Saturday Billy was right in the forefront of the bairns, face shining, cowslick combed, his jersey rumpled at the foot to conceal the yawning hole which was somehow its permanent feature.

'I've stopped swearing,' he announced triumphantly. 'I've been at the Sunday School. Jesus Christ, our-Lord-and-Saviour—That's no' swearin' now, is it?'

Gravely I conceded the point. His blue eyes danced. 'Can I come in the boat now?'

'Yes Billy, you can come in the boat'. I picked him up by the scruff of the neck and the well-worn seat of the pants and chucked him into the well. He grinned at me confidentially.

'If little Sheila as much as tries a swear, I'll gie' her h***! I mean, I'll blecken baith her een!' he amended hastily.

What has become of Billy? Alas, I do not know. To many he was just an unlovable, illegitimate little tramp. To me he was good, God-sent material, only in need of firm kindness. How very much I hope it has come his way.

October 1954

13

I started my schooling in Lerwick on the Shetland Islands where my father was stationed during the war.

That same Billy used to bully me. My father told me the next time it happened I had to punch him right on the nose. I have no memory of this daring act having taken place, but it is alleged to have happened. Blood spurted from Billy's nose and he ran away. Later he was to complain to my father—'Your Stewart bloodied my nose!' My father told him that he was lucky no worse happened to him at my hands. Was this what my father meant by 'firm kindness', I wonder?

The Luckless Loon!

QUIET CORNER

I AM THE worst person in the whole world! No, don't hasten politely to contradict me—or to exert your prior claim. I repeat, I am the worst person in the world—to one small boy at least. He delivers our morning paper and recently it has been so late that one day I challenged him.

'Look here, what's wrong?' I demanded. 'The paper used to be on the dot at 7.30. It's never here now before ten-past eight!'

'I'm sorry, mister,' he said quietly. 'I only started this week. I don't know the streets and the lad who was to show me is at the "tatties". I'll try to dae better tomorrow!'

Conscience smote me. I looked at him, small, neat though shabby, censuring me with the very straightness of his answer. His first week at work, and I was making it memorably miserable. I made some amends and wish it had been more cordial, for yesterday morning the milkman rang the bell. 'Here's anither bottle o' milk,' he said, grinning. 'The paper loon was in sic a hurry he kicked it ower. Ye'd better get a cloot!' In the distance a small figure was scurrying like Tam o' Shanter's mare . . . .

Today the paper dropped into the hallway with the softest plop, at 7.00 am. What it cost my young friend to rise at chilly dawn, to revise his unfamiliar round and to deposit that paper before the 'ogre' was awake, I shall never know.

This I do know. I don't care tuppence about a shattered bottle of milk—or is it sevenpence-ha'penny? Neither do I care about the morning's news to the extent of making a little lad's life a burden. I shall make a point of seeing him and putting his 'ogre' impression in, I trust, a slightly truer focus.

In passing, may I always be as ready as my little luckless loon to admit a fault and say: 'But I'll try to dae better tomorrow!'

October 1953

As I have said before, I have very few pictures of my father and even fewer of the two of us together. Of the odd picture or two which I *do* have, boats seem to appear. My father and mother had enjoyed a holiday in their younger days on the Norfolk Broads  when my father had managed to sail a yacht, and one of the relatives of my grandfather on my mother's side had been a sea-going captain. Sailing however does not run in *my* veins.

I remember to this day the trouble I had getting this little pleasure pond boat turned around in time for the holiday photographer to take a picture of father and son. You can see the tension in my face. Getting things done fast enough was quite often a problem for me in my young life!

◊

Speaking of Bowler Hats

AT A Command HQ when war was over, we had a pompous old Air Commodore who was such a confounded nuisance that, regularly, to get him out of the way a bit, he was packed off in a plane down the Nile valley to make voluminous reports that no one in their sane senses would ever look at. Although he served no purpose that anyone could lay a precise finger upon, he wasn't a bad old stick, and it was always our Air Commodore I thought of when I read that a batch of officers were to be 'bowler-hatted,' or—less politely—sacked.

My ideas changed recently when I met a bowler-hatted officer for whom life had suddenly assumed a grave and sombre complexion. Disregarding the anomaly of moaning about lack of recruits whilst you sack men in the prime of life, this man was given a brief university refresher course, and pump-handled by jolly rehabilitation people who begged him not to take the first thing that came along —and then promptly forgot him!

Saddened, I learned about the dead-end job he had drifted into. Tight-lipped he told me of its daily humiliations, frustrations, the near swindles he must passively countenance to earn his little family's bread.

Have you got a good job? No matter how hard you are worked, can you look on your boss with deep respect, with affection? Then spare a thought for a bowler-hatted officer who would give the world just to stand in your shoes. If, dear reader, you are like the Centurion who can say to one man, come, and he cometh, and to another, go, and he goeth, could you perhaps give this man a hearing? Could you give him a hearing now—before the bowler hat begins to become shabby?

February 1958

16

Don't Quit

When things go wrong as
they sometimes will,
when the road you're trudging
seems all up hill,
when funds are low,
and the debts are high,
and you want to smile
but you have to sigh,

when care is pressing you
down a bit—
rest if you must,
but don't you quit.

Success is failure turned
    inside out,
the silver tint of the
clouds of doubt,
and you never can tell
how close you are,
it may be near
when it seems afar.
So stick to the fight
when you are hardest hit,
it's when things go wrong
that you mustn't quit.

Anon

Tame Ducks

There are three tame ducks in our backyard
dabbling in mud and trying hard
to get their share and maybe more
of the overflowing barnyard store,
satisfied with the task they're at
of eating and sleeping and getting fat.
But, whenever the free wild ducks go by,
in a long line streaming across the sky,
they cock a quizzical eye
and flap their wings and try to fly.

I think my soul is a tame old duck
dabbling around in a barnyard muck,
fat and lazy with useless wings.
But sometimes when the north wind sings
and the wild ones hurtle overhead,
it remembers something lost and dead
and cocks a wary, bewildered eye
and makes a feeble attempt to fly.
It's fairly content with the state it's in
But it isn't the duck it might have been.

Anon

18

After the war my father never managed to re-establish himself in his writing career. Its promising start had allowed him to risk acquiring a mortgage for the house he and my mother lived in for the 40 years of their marriage.

He was a self-taught man with no formal education. After the war he went to work in an office, obtained promotion, and then they closed the office. He became a salesman of pandrops and literally worked for sweeties. But he did so with drive and energy. More pandrops were consumed in his area than had been consumed there prior to his arrival.

Later he offered his services as a 'representative' for a paint brush firm. He couldn't give them a reference but he did, with stealth, remove the books of his before and after sales figures. He told the interviewing panel that he knew little about paint brushes but if they wanted their sales figures to similarly increase, he would make that happen. They did and he did.

All his life he regretted not having become the duck he might have been. He did what he could however to give his son that chance.

The Little Lady of the Tuck Shop

QUIET CORNER

SHE IS dead now, the little lady of the Tuck Shop, but don't imagine this will be a depressing article on that account. Her little tuck shop opposite the gates of a famous academy in central Scotland was a drab enough place; the austerity of sweet rationing rendered it drabber still. But I for one would not exchange its new, freshly-painted glory and well-filled shelves for the tuck shop as it was run by this little lady—sharp-tongued, bright-eyed, alert as a sparrow, a legend of affection and awe to a generation of youths, far-flung across the bosom of the earth, whom she ruled with a rod of iron, and ever thought and spoke of privately as 'ma laddies'.

With sweets severely on points, she had a minute allocation of chocolate. Generally speaking, you had to be an ex-enemy alien to prosper in this respect. So her pathetic little stock had to be augmented by such off-points luxuries as liquorice straps, 'fizzy squibs', highly-coloured gob-stoppers, all dear to youthful palates as they were doubtful in nutritional content.

Inevitably, being a disciplinarian herself, she identified herself loosely with the teaching staff. She could quell a near-riot in a matter of moments and I well remember her indignation when someone, who should have known better, suggested teasingly, she should stock sugarelly pipes and sweetie cigarettes. 'Ma laddies'll learn nae bad habits in this shop!' was her version of the perfect squelch.

Alas, one slippy morning she had a fall and broke her leg. She was in hospital for quite a time. The shop was closed and well-meaning people took it upon themselves to write to her suppliers and cancel her chocolate allocations.

On my next trip something made me pass down her street and there, standing at the door of the open shop, pale and shaken, supported by a stick, was the little lady herself! What a state she was in. She was ready and willing to serve her laddies, but there was nothing in the place but 'fizzy squibs' and some flattened and unambitious packets of potato crisps. She could have written to her suppliers? Of course she could, but she was a very old lady, remember, and her way was to stand at the door of the shop, wring her hands and tell her tale of desolation to any passer-by.

I wrote to her chocolate firm and received an immediate reply, 'that in the very special circumstances, etc,' everything would be made all right.

She did not live much longer. She had less sparkle; she was frailer, much subdued. Yet how grateful I was to be able to do something for a rearguard member of a generation which has gone, a gracious little person who had the charm and fragrance of lavender and old lace.

September 1959

◊

The Slippy Stane

A MINISTER was polishing his sermon. 'How oft we feel that half-formed wish within us . . .' he declaimed. It was a doddle. He had it off pat. Came Sunday—'How oft we feel that half-warmed fish within us!' he thundered—to a congregation convulsed.

Psychology blames subconscious dwelling upon an unsatisfactory breakfast. I blame—the Slippy Stane.

Ministers—and their wives—must know all there is to know about the Slippy Stane. So does anyone who dabbles in print. I remember when technical difficulties were beginning to dispel and the Magazine was becoming a magazine. My mind should have been on better things, but as I approached the kirk, I recall thinking, 'It's really not bad. Someone might even say they like it.' Alas, all I got was a sound dressing-down for a name mis-spelt. That Slippy Stane again!

But the Slippy Stane has its definite use. It reminded me that Sabbath thoughts should be on Sabbath matters. It has this virtue that since it lies, as the old song says, 'at ilka body's door,' it surely becomes us all to be more kindly, more tolerant—less vinegary—one toward another.

> '*Then gently scan your brither man,*
> *Still gentler, sister woman.*
> *Tho' they may gang a' kennin' wrang,*
> *To step aside is human!*'

February 1955

21

How true, but not easy to live out, even regarding how we treat our own children.

I remember the first time I read a lesson at a Sunday Service. I was about 15 years of age. My father and mother sat in the gallery to watch and to listen to me. By evening my father had said not a word. I asked —'Don't you have anything to say about this morning?' 'Do you want me to?' my father replied. His comment was simple and direct. 'If you cannot be heard behind a ha'penny biscuit, don't speak!' That was it. He had given me his advice. Inaudibility has rarely been one of my problems since that day!

Similarly when I wrote things for *The Wyvern*, he would return my first efforts with a line through them. He grudgingly accepted my fourth or fifth effort when he knew there would be no more.

He taught me two things—a good thing: don't be content with your first efforts—and a bad thing: never be content with what you do. The latter is a parental curse, of possible life-long duration. He did not mean to impart the curse, just as I have not intentionally done so to my own children. We were doing our best. But when you look around you, you discover many victims of victims who have much to unlearn.

How Wrong Can Parents Be?

QUIET CORNER

'EACH MAN kills the thing he loves.' It is Oscar Wilde's bitterest saying. It perfectly fits a successful business man who lives far from here. Ambition, the spur, has given him every material thing; he is the most dejected of men. He despises his wife, who used to work beside him in the office, till membership of the snootier business men's clubs made this beneath his dignity. Now they have grown apart. He has forged ahead in business; with nothing to do since the family grew up, his wife has one pitiful object in life—to be the best-dressed woman in her own particular clique. As he puts it scornfully, she has nothing in her head but clothes and coffee mornings, the kind you dare not be absent from. The absentee is certain to be torn to shreds by the polite, perfumed, venomous wolf pack! Once she was the sweet companion of his business and marriage —surely it is at least as much his fault if she has become a selfish, dress-consumed, discontented drone. Most assuredly he has killed the thing he loved.

It is the attitude of his family which worries him most. His married son lives less than 20 miles away in the magnificent bungalow which was his father's gift. They could be in touch in 15 minutes in the sleek grey Jaguar, again a father's gift on the birth of his grandson. He has scarcely seen them since New Year! Even the telephone is silent. He is puzzled by his son's indifference. After all, he bought him a comfortable partnership. He signed a generous cheque so that they could tour Europe last year. It does not even occur to him that for his son and daughter-in-law he has destroyed all need to scrape and save—and grow closer in the process. He has cancelled out all joy and pride of achievement. Why is the precious grandson kept almost deliberately away? The son is resolved, perhaps unconsciously, that *his* son is to be kept as far as possible from the all-destroying Midas touch!

Only through young Susan, the daughter, have I any hope for our successful business man. With sturdy independence, Susan has spurned leisured uselessness in her mother's pattern and has gone through art school on a modest allowance. To her father's bewilderment, she has left her elaborate home for the splendid discomfort of a minute flat. She is engaged to a fellow student and they are happily scraping every penny towards possessing their own small art and antique shop. Need I tell you—her father has offered to buy one, lock, stock and barrel, and again, to his utter bewilderment, he has met with polite but firm refusal. They will be poor as church mice, but they will be radiantly happy. Wise little Susan. In her own way she is trying to tell her father that the cloying Midas touch which turns everything merely to money, can rob life of all its fine endeavour, all romance, all joy in personal achievement. 'Each man kills the thing he loves.' I pray that my friend will be spared the indignity of destroying Susan's splendid independence. It is a pearl of price, the last of his worthwhile possessions.

August 1964

23

Children Learn What They Live

If a child lives with criticism,
    He learns to condemn.
If a child lives with hostility,
    He learns to fight.
If a child lives with ridicule,
    He learns to be shy.
If a child lives with shame,
    He learns to feel guilty.
If a child lives with tolerance,
    He learns to be patient.
If a child lives with encourage-
        ment,
    He learns confidence.
If a child lives with praise,
    He learns to appreciate.
If a child lives with fairness,
    He learns justice.
If a child lives with security,
    He learns to have faith.
If a child lives with approval,
    He learns to like himself.
If a child lives with acceptance
    and friendship, he learns
        to find love in the world.

Anon

For the children of my congregation I used to write 'Dougal' stories. The one below is based on a dialogue which took place between my then 10 year old daughter and myself in the manse in Bellfield.

It took me 17 years and 1 month to learn to listen to my son. One evening I had been able to give someone caring, listening attention for four hours. Earlier that evening I had not managed to give Stewart four *minutes*! The following evening I started to listen to my son.

Up to then I had told him what *I* wanted for him—regarding friends, clothes, schoolwork (something he was averse to) and so on. I had pleaded with him, warned him, bribed him to work harder. I had rained advice on his head—good advice, caring advice, from an older and wiser head—but I hadn't listened to him. I had been trying to do *for* him rather than be *with* him. Happily we, too, became good pals. During my illness he has demonstrated a remarkable ability to be *with* his father, something I achieved only at the end of my own father's life.

Good Pals

Mum and Marybell had gone out shopping, leaving Dad and Dougal to spend the afternoon together.

It was a lovely summer day and the two of them were out in the garden. When the ice-cream van came round they bought two cones and sat on the grass eating them.

'We're good pals, aren't we Dad?' said Dougal.

'Yes, we are', said Dad.

'Do you know what the best thing about it is, Dad?' Dougal asked.

His Dad thought for a moment.

What on earth did Dougal mean?

Was it the holidays they had enjoyed together?

Or the fun they had together playing with Dougal's model railway?

Had it anything to do with Dougal getting a new bike?

'What do you mean, Dougal?' asked Dad.

Dougal replied—'We can always tell each other how we feel, Dad'.

During my illness the singer of my son's favourite pop song tells how he knew himself to be a prisoner to all his father held dear; he felt himself a hostage to all his father's hopes and fears and he tells of how he wishes that he had been able to tell his father, *in the living years*, just exactly how he had felt.

Life's Lessons

After a while you learn the difference between holding a hand and chaining a soul. You learn that love isn't leading, but lending support.

You begin to accept your defeats with the grace of an adult, not the grief of a child.

You decide to build your roads on today, for tomorrow's ground is too uncertain.

You help someone to plant a garden instead of waiting for someone to bring you flowers.

You learn that God has given you the strength to endure and that you really do have worth.

Anon

◇
Gossip—The Unlovely Thing

'WHAT DOES she think she is? Her that went tae Coogate Skale—jeely piece an' a' . . . and her faither naething but a mill stour!'

This little fragment in the Cowgate the other day clearly denoted that someone was getting a round of the guns. Gossip—it is a most unlovely thing. We are all guilty of it, but not, let us hope, to the following extent.

A very young wife was living quietly, longing for the day when her sailor husband would come home from sea. At last he did return and the young bride, for she was scarcely more, fairly came to life.

They went here and there; her step was light, her smile ecstatic. At length the dream leave ended, and he returned to his ship.

It was at Port Said that the letter reached her husband, unsigned, anonymous—like all good gossip. 'There is something we think you should know. Your wife has been seen . . . .' The long and short of it was that in time, place and personal appearance, the husband recognised himself, and the incidents of their treasured leave together!

The incident did end in laughter between them, but

27

the young wife said soberly afterwards: 'Just think, someone, or some people around here, would go to that extent to make trouble . . . and yet they all appear so friendly!'

I like to reflect the withering scorn the gossips must have met when they carried their tales to Christ. 'Lord have you heard what they are saying about Mary Magdalene?'

Christ loathed gossip—and it was gossip and the kindred sins of malice and envy which finally killed our Lord. 'What does he think he is. . . and his faither naething but a carpenter!' *His Father!*

I sometimes think we could kill gossip with a bored, glassy stare, indicating that as far as we are concerned it has reached a terminus.

I do like the bit in our minister's recent play 'The Lamb', when Daara has her withered arm restored. She is incoherent at first, then in joy and gratitude she exclaims: 'I will use it to do good to everyone!'

December 1953

I wonder how many of the many, many people, whom Jesus helped and healed, made and kept Daara's promise. I wonder how many were envious of him—*'What does he think he is? And his faither naething but a carpenter!'*

As the quote by H G Wells (on the next page) explains, many people must have felt threatened by Jesus.

A long time earlier through his spokesman Jeremiah, God had promised: *'The time is coming when I will make a new covenant with the people Israel . . . .*

I will be their God and they will be my people . . . all will know me, From the least to the greatest . . . .

I will no longer remember their wrongs.' (Jeremiah 31:31 ff)

Excitement was high about this when Jesus, following carefully laid plans, rode into Jerusalem, calling to mind another Old Testament passage—Zechariah 9:9f. Like the people in the QUIET CORNER above, many on Palm Sunday saw only what they wanted to see—the promised time, the promised leader. However, the promised purpose they did not see.

Is It Any Wonder?

'Is it any wonder that the priests realised that between this man and themselves there was no chance but that he or witchcraft should perish?

'Is it any wonder that the Roman soldiers, confronted and amazed by something soaring over their comprehensions and threatening all their disciplines, should take refuge in wild laughter and crown him with thorns, and robe him in purple to make a mock Caesar of him?

'For to take him seriously was to enter upon a strange and alarming life, to abandon habits, to control instincts and impulses, to essay an incredible happiness.'

H G Wells

Thirty Pieces of Silver

QUIET CORNER

SIR WALTER SCOTT'S two horses, bearing him on his last journey to Dryburgh Abbey, stopped without human prompting at the familiar view of the Tweed which their master had loved so well.

Rab, a collie, was devoted to his tiny mistress and followed her everywhere. When she fell into the river and was swept away, Rab instantly plunged in after her, keeping her head above water as he paddled them both to the bank. This proved too steep. Still keeping his little friend and precious burden above water, Rab turned downstream, bringing her safely ashore on a sandy strip, from where he actually tried to drag her home.

What is the reward for Rab? A history book mention like Sir Walter's horses, an honoured old age, his gallantry ever remembered? No—the very next week the girl's father sold him to a shepherd for thirty shillings!

Gallant Rab, doubtless he tackled his strange, unfamiliar tasks with the same stout heart which sent him plunging into the boiling stream after his little friend. At least, as a dog he is spared the pang of knowing about the greater Betrayal—for Thirty Pieces of Silver.

January 1978

What cruel people did to Jesus meant a lot to the writer of QUIET CORNER. He was acutely aware of man's ingratitude and unkindness.

The faithful in Israel, trusting in the love and care of God, looked to God to establish a new covenant, a new relationship, a new beginning for his people.

On the Thursday of Holy Week, at a carefully prepared meal in an upper room with his disciples, Jesus gave them 'an illustrated word of God' (Brunner).

He took a loaf of bread, broke it and said—'This is my body, broken for you'. He knew what was about to happen.

Later in the meal he gave them a cup of wine and said—'This cup is God's new covenant sealed with my blood which is poured out for you.

At St Ninian's, Bellfield, we held evening services throughout Holy Week. On the Thursday we held a pre-crucifixion commemoration of the Last Supper—enacting that moving illustrated word of God.

The service ended with the words—'And when they had sung a hymn they went out into the night'— and our choir sang 'All in the April Evening', something which I had first heard in the congregation of my upbringing.

All In The April Evening

All in the April evening
April airs were abroad;
The sheep with their little lambs
Passed me by on the road;
All in the April evening
I thought on the Lamb of God.
The lambs were weary and crying
with a weak human cry;
I thought on the Lamb of God
going meekly to die.

Up in the blue, blue mountains
Dewy pastures are sweet;
Rest for the little bodies
Rest for the little feet.
But for the Lamb, the Lamb of God
up on the hill top green,
only a cross, a cross of shame,
Two stark crosses between.

All in the April evening,
April mists were abroad;
I saw the sheep with their lambs
And thought on the Lamb of God.

Hugh S Robertson

◊

On a Spring Morning

ON A Spring morning three trees whispered together.

Said the first—'I should like to be fashioned into a baby's cradle. How lovely that would be'. The second said—'I should like to become a great ship and bring fine cargos from the ends of the earth'. The third murmured dreamily in the pleasant breeze, 'I should like to be left here looking up at heaven all day and pointing men to God'.

Men came and cut down the first tree and fashioned it, not into a dainty cradle, as it had hoped, but into a rude manger and common beasts ate out of it. But when the infant Jesus was born, he was placed in that very manger and it kept him snug and warm.

They cut down the second tree and instead of making it into a stately ship, they made just a plain and sturdy fishing craft. But Jesus did not scorn to preach from it and from it commanded the raging sea to be still.

They came across the third tree and said—'We shall make this one into a cross.' The tree cried out in protest. 'But I don't want to be a cross. That's a thing thieves and murderers die on! I won't be a cross, I tell you . . . .'

They made a cross of the tree, and on another spring morning men in their sin and foolishness hung Jesus upon it to die a painful, lingering death. And because it became a cross, the tree to this day points men upwards to God.

April 1957

32

'Jesus' first followers walked many a mile with him as he healed the sick and strove to set people free from their chains. They shared many a dangerous moment with him as he shared his faith, his enthusiasm for life and the kingdom of God. They watched his physical body cruelly beaten and then broken on a cross. Confusion and utter despair followed this sight but soon they came to experience and know that his life-giving ministry had not come to an end. They knew he wanted them to share his continuing ministry.

'The Spirit-filled transformation in their lives was amazing. They became convinced of his call to them to go to all the inhabitants of God's 'garden' and of his promise to be with them in their faith-sharing.

'And so an enthusiastic new movement came into being—the Christian Church—a people with a purpose (a mission) to share with the world:

- New eyes with which to see.
- New ears with which to listen.
- New minds to understand life.
- New hearts to love and trust and risk.

'The New Testament often describes the Church as "the body of Christ"—an awesome term when we think of what Jesus' physical body had to endure.'

(The above is an extract from one of my books which I would have liked my father to have seen, entitled *Caring for God's People*, co-written with Ken Lawson, The Saint Andrew Press, 1989.)

St Ninian's, Bellfield
A local church and its buildings should
*symbolise God's care for **all** his people.*

'The Minister is Ower Dramatic!'

NO, I AM not writing about Mr Campbell, although I confess to using one of the oldest journalistic dodges to ensure that you will read my little piece. It concerns a far-off parish, where an acquaintance of mine was excusing himself to me—to *me*, mark you—for not attending his village kirk.

'I'd like to go,' he said. 'I'd go like a shot, too, but yon craitur in the poolpit fair gi'es you the creeps. Forbye sending you to sleep, you wouldna' hear him ahent a ha'penny biscuit!'

Time rolled on. The minister who, allegedly, was silent behind his abernethy biscuit, was gathered unmourned to his fathers, and I read in the country newspaper that a young, brisk fellow had taken his place.

This was the stuff to give them. Surely now my friend would be pleased. I asked him about it. Wariness fought with shame upon his countenance—and wariness won.

'Aye, we've got a new lad in the poolpit,' he said drily. 'Mind you, I've only heard him once—at communion. No, I havena' gone back. I'd like to, you ken, but yon new lad o' ours—he's far ower dramatic.'

Snuggle down below the blankets on a Sunday morning; reach cosily for the Sunday papers vieing with each other in spicy salacity. Although we only grace the kirk with our presence on the rarest of occasions, we need never be at loss for an alibi, novel, plaintive, unassailable—'the Minister is ower dramatic!'

May 1960

Ah, so that's where my father got his 'ha'penny biscuit' saying from! His QUIET CORNERS were often directed at those who neglected Sunday worship. Whether or not he made up the 'Devil's Beatitudes' which follow, I'm not sure.

The Devil's Beatitudes

BLESSED ARE they who are too busy to assemble with the congregation on Sunday; for they are my best workers.

Blessed are they who complain loudly that their minister is 'too dramatic': they will get nothing out of the sermon.

Blessed is the Church member who expects to be invited to his own Church: for he is important to me.

Blessed are they who come to church only at Communion: they cause the world to say with truth—'The Church is falling off'.

Blessed are they who are touchy and easily offended: for they get angry and quit.

Blessed are they who do not regularly support God's work and mission: they help me to apply the brake.

Blessed is he who professes to love God but hates his brother: he will be with me for ever.

Blessed are the trouble-makers: for they shall be called the children of the Devil.

Blessed is he who has no need to pray: he shall be my prey to all eternity.

May 1979

The Great Renewal

Cardinal Cushing wrote this crisp little verse:

> 'If all the sleeping folk will wake up,
> All the lukewarm folk fire up,
> All the crooked folk straighten up,
> All the depressed folk cheer up,
> All the estranged folk make up,
> All the gossip-folk shut up,
> All the dry bones shake up,
> All true believers stand up,
> All church members show up
> To honour Him who was lifted up,
> Then we can have the world's greatest renewal.'

October 1977

Ladies of the Lamp

'REMEMBER, REMEMBER—'. In my case, since I cannot eat a boiled egg unaided and will not drive my car for weeks, it is the Fourth of November that sticks in my mind. In capturing a young marauder on neighbouring premises, I met with an accident and in a matter of minutes—life can be as sudden as that—I was on my way to Dundee Royal Infirmary.

As a ratepayer, have you looked askance at the bills for replacing the bumpy old 'cassies' of Dundee with smooth, modern roads? One trip by ambulance, even when driven with brotherly caution, with a broken shoulder and collar bone, and you would advocate that all the rough places be made smooth with the least possible delay!

So there I was at the Infirmary. After years of being on the outside, looking in, I was for a few hours on the inside looking out.

How would things be under the National Health? Would doctors be callous to pain, nurses indifferent? I can say little about the doctors since their labours did not call for my conscious participation. But I can speak of the nurses. If every young soldier has in his knapsack a Field Marshal's baton, then quite reasonably every young nurse has, somewhere among her possessions, a Lamp of Florence Nightingale.

In coming as one more bedraggled stranger from the night into the hands of the Little Ladies of Night Casualty, X-ray and Ward 14, I can personally vouch that their lamps of selfless devotion and kindly service are not merely lit, but are well-trimmed and brightly burning.

November 1958

36

I remember this evening well. I was enjoying a bath when my father fell injured through the front door. I remember how only one ambulanceman was sent and I had to help carry my father on his stretcher. I also remember the bumpy ride very well—and my 'discussion' with the father of the 'young marauder' later that evening.

The Sheep with their Lambs

QUIET CORNER

I AM DEEPLY impressed by those people who write to the newspapers, dutifully reporting each spring that they have heard the first cuckoo. I am impressed, because in all the matchless melody of Earth's awakening, I cannot honestly claim I have ever heard the cuckoo!

But how I watch for the lambs. I pity the over-punctual, ushered into an inhospitable world of ice and snow. I smile at happier groups, romping in the sunshine and finding the warm earth a radiant, wondrous place.

I saw my first lambs this year just west of Methven. Not one or two, but scores of them on the first spring-like day, accompanying their mothers to pasture.

Now, indeed, the shepherd's dog must be upon his mettle. Technique is different. Feigned fierceness and a series of determined rushes are no use with these tiny, teetering creatures, whose silly legs never bear them for three consecutive moments in one direction. A dog must be everywhere at once.

Not every sheep is docile. Watch that ewe who senses indignity in the marshalling of her lambkin. With lowered head she goes twice, three times for its tormentor. The dog skips lightly out of the way. Not so the lamb which, in all this turmoil, tumbles precipitately into the ditch!

A husky summons—it is not a bark—brings the second dog at the double. Now both are under the bleating lamb which, thinking its

last day has about coincided with its first, forgets to struggle and is the more easily prised up and out by a concerted pincer movement.

May 1956

Contentment

QUIET CORNER

I SEE few films and remember fewer, but one in particular I did enjoy. It was called 'If I had a Million', and dealt with the reactions of widely differing people to whom the random choice of a wealthy crank brought the amazing windfall of a million dollars!

To Charles Laughton, ageing, down-trodden clerk, it spelt freedom. Receiving the news like an electric shock, he actually left his desk without permission, to traverse corridor after corridor, past under-secretaries, vice-presidents, to enter, unannounced, the very inner sanctum and there deliver to the architect of a lifetime's degradation—an outer size in 'raspberries'.

To a young lady of more charm than virtue, wealth purchased the means to place an entire hotel suite between herself and the nearest wolf call. A condemned killer could not be dissuaded that wealth beyond avarice—beyond the impulse to kill for a dollar or two—would *not* spare him the bitter pangs of the death walk to the electric chair!

Yes, money can buy many desirable things, but it is not the currency of contentment. Great writers have sought to define contentment. I humbly submit it is simply the ability to enjoy simple things.

If you have a measure of health; if you have a wife who is tolerant and kind, relatives with whom you can agree—or agree to differ—be content. No need to seek hypothetical pots of gold at the end of ephemeral rainbows.

You have in your very fingers as much of the precious stuff of contentment as this restless world is likely to afford.

April 1954

For various reasons life provided my father with a limited supply of money. He felt bad about not being able to provide for his wife like other relatives did by way of clothes and holidays for their wives. By great self-denial he and my mother spent a lot of money on my education. To my father education was a treasure. He had been given little of it as a boy. He did not want his son to miss out on formal education. Trying to succeed I found to be emotionally costly. I was, however, never conscious of him counting a single penny of the financial cost of the education he and my mother gave me at a private school. He was a generous man.

He and my mother could be content pottering around the garden together in the summer months. Looking at him, sun-tanned in his old khaki shorts, you would have thought him some eccentric inhabitant of tropical climes.

I remember one day after he had retired, we were in the town of Ayr. I had to work hard to try to persuade him to spend a couple of pounds on an item which he didn't actually need, but which he wanted for himself.

$\Diamond$

Tribute to Dorothy

I HAVE been in the midst of sorrow in recent days. It is only hours since I held the hand of the distracted mother who lost her bairn in the Train Crash: of the incredibly brave young widow who lost her husband. Before that, I stood by the earthly remains of Dorothy, a deeply respected young niece, who lived a year and seven days after being knocked down by a lorry.

I write so often about little things that happen as I travel the country. Bear with me as I pay heartfelt tribute to a girl you probably did not know, but who earned the admiration of surgeons, doctors, nurses and a host of friends by the gallant, even cheerful, at all times uncomplaining struggle against injury, too severe for mortal frame.

Why do they happen, these things which test our belief and let scoffers say—'What God would let them happen?' We have to accept it that there is risk in almost every aspect of daily life. Children are dear for the very reason that they are frail, born of suffering and subject to death.

But why Dorothy? Why one who was so young, so good, so light of heart? In my own experience I have more than once seen untimely death beckon to young people of unusual merit—as though their task here was done sooner than the rest of us. 'Age shall not weary them, nor the years condemn . . . .'

Of one thing I am certain. As Dorothy died at midnight, her soul did not flicker and go out into utter loss and darkness. On this quiet Sunday afternoon she is happier than we are, and only grieved in the measure that her loved ones are grieving over her.

June 1955

40

⸳Tribute to Gordon

QUIET CORNER

SUNDAY 18th October—pre-Communion Sunday—last day of the golden summer which has lingered incredibly into late October. We were scarcely back from church when there came the astounding news from Nigeria that Gordon Gilchrist, well-known, well-liked young husband of our own Moira Simpson, had lost his life in a boating tragedy at Lagos.

Many of us were at their wedding; many more will remember the handsome, smiling sailor who used to wait shyly for Moira at the gates—until he plucked up courage at last to come inside and discuss wedding arrangements!

Beyond average, Gordon Gilchrist was full of the joy and zest for living. In a roomful of people, attention would centre upon him as he sparked off the entire company with his wit, his infectious gaiety, his abounding fun and good spirits. He lived each day to the full; he had no time for moping or melancholy. Fearless, adventurous, generous to a fault, it is no surprise to learn that in mortal danger he relinquished the rope which would have secured his own life, and threw it to a friend.

From the recent home-coming, memories throng back of Gordon happily taking movie pictures of every youngster in sight; Gordon bearing with swelling joy and pride his charming little daughter as she received her name in St Andrew's Church. Gordon served two churches. It was his recent wish, however, to join St Andrew's which had witnessed the two happiest ceremonies of his life—his wedding and the christening of Baby Eileen.

The Gilchrist and Simpson families, though not of St Andrew's, enjoy the high regard and affection of many of our people. To them

41

we offer heartfelt St Andrew's sympathy. Even as I write Moira is winging her way home to the care and comfort of those who love her best. Her we commend to the tenderness and solace of Almighty God. Who alone can wipe away every tear; Who alone can restore to us at the Great Home-coming dear ones, deeply loved and lost but for a while.

November 1959

My Friend Tracy

LET ME tell you about my delightful encounter with Tracy. Tracy is an enchanting little soul, perhaps four years of age. I was waiting for her Daddy in Fraserburgh. Her Mummy was preparing tea. Tracy and I were in the sitting-room and clearly she felt it was her place to entertain me.

'Sit down,' she said, and sat opposite me.

'What is your name?'

I explained—plain John.

'I've got a boyfriend,' she confided, this little mite of four. 'He's called John too, and he's a butcher—at Cooper's'.

I was duly impressed.

'Have you got a little boy?' she asked next.

I said not exactly, our son was actually a biggish minister in Kilmarnock.

'Have you got a little girl like me, then? NO! WHY?'

So I chattered with this uninhibited, charming, friendly little maid, of whom I have thought often with a smile in these recent weeks.

As we parted, I remembered that Jesus himself said—'Of such is the Kingdom of God'.

October 1978

42

'I Know Where Jesus Works!'

VALERIE is a lovely child. Valerie is only four. In due course parental decree will gently insist that I must enjoy avuncular status and to Valerie I shall become just one more honorary and relatively unimportant 'uncle'. Meantime, in her dewy and tender innocence she calls me 'John'. I am her friend, confidant and perfect equal. The arrangement suits me perfectly.

Quite apart from regular entertainment provided by her latest batch of sayings, Valerie has just presented me with the very finest child story I have ever heard.

Valerie is used to grace being said before meals in her home and by way of explanation in the simplest of terms, her mummy told her that grace meant thanking Jesus for all the good things we enjoy, the consequence being that at the end of every grace Valerie adds her own particular little postscript—'Thank you, dear Jesus, for sending all our good food!'

Something of a sensation occurred at prayers the other day when Valerie suddenly announced with perfect aplomb—'Mummy, I know where Jesus works!'

Not one whit perturbed by looks of bewilderment, she volunteered the additional information. 'He wears a lovely white coat and he works in Landsburgh, the grocer's. And when you buy the food, Mummy, he always says—'No, no, Mrs Reid, that's much too heavy for you to carry. You must let me send them for you'. Now isn't Jesus such a kind man?!'

June 1960

To a June Bride!

DO YOU like weddings? I most unashamedly do. Notwithstanding the fact that as a young reporter a staff shortage pressed the men into service to 'cover' a spate of weddings and one lush effusion of mine was bannered with the strange device—'by our Lady Correspondent'.

So, of the charming June wedding we attended in Rosyth I could write with professional skill that the bride wore a creation of stiff organdie, richly appliqued in lace and all encased in net . . . .

But it is of Daureen the bride, and not her charming dress, that I am thinking. How could I feel other than tender towards her? The little girl in gym dress, the teenager I taught tennis—now pale and lovely, starry-eyed, by the side of the husband of her supremely happy choice.

A June wedding—there is special magic there. Yet the thought occurs to me that surely more faith, more hope, more courage than ever before is needed from all young people setting up their homes in this nuclear dawn, when man's feeble morality strives vainly, it seems, to restrain the monster unleashed by his own brain.

Of one thing we can be sure. Young hearts will thrill to young hearts, youth will plan golden tomorrows, marriage with all the happiness and sacredness of family life will still endure when the smoke and ashes of the last nuclear convulsions have ceased to poison the breath of this good earth.

July 1957

How my father would have enjoyed being present at my daughter Debbie's wedding. It took place some nine years too late for him. He would have enjoyed the DIY nature of the wedding—with me marrying off my own daughter and my wife making most of the dresses. He would have enjoyed the discovery that his grandson had been involved in the making of the beautiful new flower pedestals in use that day in the church for the very first time. We would have easily found for my father some part in the proceedings.

◊

The Friendly Island!

SINCE I wrote last summer of the charm of Tighnabruaich—'where the road ends'—and its entrancing view of the Kyles, I have longed to cross the narrow strip of water which separates the mainland from the Isle of Bute.

We did so on holiday this year, by the eastern limb of the Kyles, where a landing-craft ferry plies from charming Colintraive to sterner Rudhbodach. From there a mile or two of excellent road brings one to quaint Port Bannatyne and neighbouring carefree Rothesay.

Is it pure imagination, or is Bute a specially hospitable and friendly place? Is it the wonder of its scenery which makes the folk more softly spoken, more ready to smile upon the stranger who comes their way? In all the time we were there I never heard a discordant word!

Bute is a pleasant place to roam. Its bays have lilting names —Ettrick, Scalpsie, Dunagoil. Even yet, the view from the hotel gardens, past Ardmaleish and towards the Cowal Hills, which frame the Kyles, can bring back a nostalgic wave of longing to return.

May I tell you of one peerless day when a jolly party of six, with three lads, chartered a fair-sized craft from Mr Peter M McIntyre of Port Bannatyne? 'The Ghillie' is little to look at, but she has a good broad beam and a sturdy, reliable engine.

Soon we are taking a pleasant toss from the wash of the 'St Columba' and waving happily to its passengers as we beat from Ardmaleish towards Strone Point, then up the far-famed Kyles. A few minutes of apprehension while we negotiate the islands north of Bute, and a few breath-taking moments while we tackle the narrow channel between Eilean Dubh and the spur which houses Glen

45

Caladh Castle, and we enter Loch Ridden. Circling the two coasters, we go down to quarter-throttle for tea which tastes nectar-like in the brilliant sunshine. Then we chug down the other leg of the Kyles to inspect Tighnabruaich and Kames with their boats, hotels and chalets —'like a Swiss village,' someone observes, 'dreaming above an azure sea'.

How much fuel left? Plenty if we do not linger too long in this halcyon spot. Now we head for the point of the island and a spin of the wheel turns us south to Port Bannatyne again. So at last, regretfully, we tie the boat up after a gorgeous, memorable day which will be savoured again and again by our friends and ourselves when the winds of winter blow.

There is no one waiting to snatch the hire money and it is next day before we saunter down leisurely and 'pay the fare'. A great fellow is Mr McIntyre. A little thing like the hire of a boat does not put him up or down. Well he knows that the majority of people who come to this enchanted and friendly spot will want to come again!

September 1955

From a QUIET CORNER like that one you would think that my father's life had in fact had its fair quota of holidays. I doubt if he got many as a boy. His son certainly didn't. Money had to be spent on other things— like buying your own car to be a salesman for a low quality firm (before his graduation to representative status in a Christian-based firm); paying for my education at a private school (rescuing me from my failure to pass the 'eleven plus' examination); and house repairs.

My parents could make the most however of a couple of days in a good hotel, or now and again a week in simpler premises.

My own family spent a number of good holidays with my parents. My father was a self-taught lover of the French language. One year we offered to take him and my mother to Lucerne, where my family had been before, and where my father could practice his french *in situ*. We drove over a thousand miles from Kilmarnock to Lucerne in pouring rain. Sitting in his tent, his nose as always in a book, my father said, without looking up, 'Did you have to bring me all this way to sit in the rain?' I learned that we had to cross the Alps and go down into Italy if we wished sunshine and no rain. This we did and landed in a rather rough campsite largely inhabited by the women and children of Milan, joined by their menfolk at the weekends.

46

When he discovered that his grandchildren were getting a bit bullied in the campsite, my father turned his attention to an Italian/English phrase book. He taught Debbie two words to say next time she was bullied. What these words were we have no idea, but they had a remarkable effect. Perhaps they were another demonstration of his 'firm (*linguistic*) kindness'!

The Lonely Heart

QUIET CORNER

THERE IS ART in the artless attraction of friends, and Jean, who did not possess that rarest gift, found the busy art college a dreary, unfriendly place. She was depressed and miserable until one day a pretty girl greeted her with a pleasant remark in passing.

A little thing, but enough to break down the walls of indifference that so oppressed and made the lonely one feel, thrillingly, part of the order of things . . . .

Next day the same girl was tripping down the marble steps with a friend when, to her surprise, Jean stopped her, pinned a little bunch of snowdrops on her coat and with a smile turned quickly away.

The recipient of the flowers was puzzled. 'How very sweet of her, but how odd,' she said. 'After all, I've only spoken to her once.'

Her friend looked at her with sudden insight. 'Probably that was the reason. I haven't spoken to her at all!'

March 1955

My father was, I think, a lonely man. He was outgoing as a salesman and could be very caring for people. But inside of him there was a deep loneliness. Many people are part of this feeling of loneliness. The seeds of it can lie buried in our past—in the self-image, the view of other people, and of life itself which we formed when young.

My parents lived very much as a couple—looking after each other, looking after me, and keeping a roof over our heads. Most evenings and Saturday mornings my mother worked as a piano teacher, working for a pittance despite her Royal Academy degree in Music and her proud teaching record.

In the early years of their marriage my father spent his evenings making toy telephones to supplement the family income. He sold them to toy shops. Later his evenings were filled with the paperwork and planning of a good salesman. Time was also given to editing *The Wyvern* and to his other growing church interests.

He dealt with much of his loneliness and with his tensions through work. There might have been more snowdrops in his life had more of the people who knew him spent more time getting behind the façades to his inner loneliness.

Some Be-Attitudes

Blessed are those who can laugh at
themselves; they will have
endless amusement.

Blessed are those who can tell
a mountain from a molehill;
they will be spared a lot of trouble.

Blessed are those who can go to bed
and fall asleep without looking
for excuses; they will become
wise.

Blessed are those who know when to
shut up and listen; they will learn new
things thereby.

Blessed are those who are intelligent
enough not to take themselves
seriously; they will be appreciated
by those around them.

Blessed are those who are attentive
to the call of others without thinking

themselves indispensable; they will be
sowers of joy.

HAPPY are you if you know how to take
small things seriously and large things
peacefully; you will go far in life.

HAPPY are you if you can admire a smile
and forget a frown; your path will be
sunlight.

HAPPY are you if you can keep quiet
and smile, even when someone
cuts you off in mid-sentence, when
someone contradicts you, when
someone treads on your toes;
the Gospel is beginning to penetrate
your heart.

Blessed above all are you if you can
recognise the lord in everyone
you meet; you have the true light
and true wisdom.

Anon

$\lozenge$

A Thought for Harvest-Time

IN WARTIME, a church in London was all set to celebrate its Harvest Thanksgiving the following day. There was a truly fine display with, as its centre-piece, a full sheaf of corn.

On Saturday night, however, the bombers came and by morning the entire church was a heap of ruins.

Months passed, winter ended and spring returned. On the bomb site where God's Church had been, there emerged a great patch of green shoots. All summer they grew and grew till in the autumn there was a flourishing patch of corn. In a night of holocaust the seeds of the sheaf of corn had sown themselves. Not all the bombs, the devastation, the ruin could extinguish the life that God gave the corn.

Life is always stronger than death, though death with its seeming finality would seem to have supremacy.

Jesus said—'Because I live, you will live also.' (John 14:19)

September 1978

I remember when I was a boy drawing with a pencil on a scrap of paper. I am no artist. At the left-hand side there was a hand—God's hand, God's life-giving hand.

OUR LIFE'S JOURNEY COMES FROM GOD.

From the hand I drew a line, a wavy line of ups and downs, with match-stick figures, representing my boyhood awareness of life's ups and downs. The line ended with another hand—God's hand, God's receiving hand.

OUR LIFE'S JOURNEY MOVES TOWARDS GOD.

I should have connected the two hands in an embrace, representing GOD'S CONTINUOUS PRESENCE.

Footprints

One night a man had a dream. He dreamed he was walking along the beach with the LORD. Across the sky flashed scenes from his life. For each scene, he noticed two sets of footprints in the sand; one belonging to him, and the other to the LORD.

When the last scene of his life flashed before him, he looked back at the footprints in the sand. He noticed that many times along the path of his life there was only one set of footprints. He also noticed that it happened at the very lowest and saddest times in his life.

This really bothered him and he questioned the LORD about it: 'LORD, you said that once I decided to follow you, you'd walk

with me all the way. But I have noticed that during the most troublesome times in my life, there is only one set of footprints. I don't understand why when I needed you most you would leave me.'

The LORD replied, 'My precious, precious child, I love you and I would never leave you. During your times of trial and suffering, when you see only one set of footprints, it was *then* that I carried you'.

Anon

My Little Lady's Hands

THE MODERN Grandma is dashing and 'with it', and I for one would not see her different. The Grandma I want to tell you about is a gracious little lady of a bygone day. Gently smiling, in flowered bonnet, necklet, voluminous skirt—hands sedately clasped outside the folds of her pretty pink shawl—she breathes the fragrance of a quieter age and is the doyen of our little group of porcelain figures.

In recent years more and more of the popular figures have been reappearing in the shops—at staggeringly increased prices. Recently I was agreeably surprised to find myself outside a shop window, face to face with 'Grandma', circa 1976. The same face, the same dress and colouring, but wait a moment—was she the same?

It was minutes before I had the answer. The shawl was now actually closed, avoiding the need for today's craftsman to bother with a trifling detail like the making of a pair of exquisite hands!

Our little old lady above the fireplace has an enhanced value; in years to come she may be a rarity indeed. She represents more than a change in fashion of dress. She reminds one of a day when detail was all-important, when no self-respecting craftsman would accept orders from cost-conscious management to cut corners, from the cynical viewpoint that 'no-one will notice the difference'.

May 1977

Does every generation look back to the previous one and lament the apparent backwards progress? Is it just a sign of getting older or are we letting standards slip—standards of excellence, craftsmanship, morality, spirituality? The fact that there is inside me the hope that 'Grandma', who now sits on *my* mantelpiece, may become a thing of enhanced value, perhaps even rarity, and so more financially valuable, points to the fact that craftsmanship is not one of my attributes or interests. I have a reputation for not being able to tie a knot in a piece of string. One of the reasons for this is that I could never tie the knot fast enough for my father. I quickly  learned that if I hung back just long enough, he would do it for me. Deskilled I was, and still remain.

Although the written word was the love of his life, my father was also skilled with his hands. He enjoyed making things—especially toys for his grandchildren. He would be proud of them—Debbie a teacher of children; Stewart Andrew (as I write) at work with a master craftsman and showing all the signs of becoming one, and one who would not miss out the hands just to cut corners.

Blessed Are They . . .

THIS POEM was found after her death in the handbag of a 98 year old lady, Mrs Janet Logie, of Buckhaven, Fife. It consisted of a scrap of paper torn from a jotter. The poem had a sensational reception when it was included in a broadcast. Its writer is unknown:

Blessed are they who understand, my faulty steps and shaky hand.
Blessed are they who know my ears today, must strain to catch the
    things they say.
Blessed are they who seem to know, my eyes are dim and my mind
    is slow.
Blessed are they who looked away, when tea was spilt on the cloth
    today.
Blessed are they with a cheery smile, who stop to chat for a little while.
Blessed are they who never say—'You've told that story twice today!'
Blessed are they who know the ways, to bring back memories of
    yesterdays.
Blessed are they who make it known, I'm loved and respected and
    not alone.
Blessed, they who know I'm at a loss, to find more strength to bear
    my Cross.
Blessed are they who ease the days, of my journey home in loving ways.

April 1979

One Sunday I heard on the radio, during a service of worship, the piece of writing which appears on the next page. I found it very moving indeed. It was also read at a Sunday morning service my wife and I attended. I think my father would have liked it and made of it a QUIET CORNER. It was written by an old lady who had been a patient in Ashludie Hospital, near Dundee. It was found in the old lady's locker after she had died.

What do you see nurses? What do you see?
Are you thinking when you look at me—
A crabbit old woman, not very wise,
Uncertain of habit, with far away eyes.
Who dribbles her food and makes no reply
When you say in a loud voice 'I do wish you'd try'.
Who seems not to notice the things that you do,
and forever is losing a stocking, a shoe.
Who, unresisting or not, lets you do as you will
With bathing or feeding, the long day to fill.
Is that what you are thinking? Is that what you see?
Then open your eyes nurse—you are not looking at me.
I'll tell you who I am as I sit here so still,
As I rise at your bidding and eat at your will.
I'm a small child of ten, with a father and mother,
Brothers and sisters who love one another;
A young girl of sixteen with wings on her feet,
Dreaming that soon now a lover she'll meet,
A bride soon at twenty, my heart gives a leap.
Remembering the vows that I promised to keep.
At twenty-five now I have young of my own,
Who need me to build a secure happy home.
A woman of thirty, my young now grow fast,
Bound to each other with ties that should last.
At forty—my young sons now grown up have gone.
But my man stays beside me to see I don't mourn.
At fifty—once more babies play at my knee,
Again we know children, my loved one and me.
Dark days are upon me, my husband is dead.
I look at the future, I shudder with dread.
For my young are all busy rearing young of their own.
And I think of the years, and the love I have known.
I'm an old woman now, and nature is cruel—
The body crumbles, grace and vigour depart.
There is now a stone where I once had a heart.
But inside this old carcase a young girl still dwells
And now and again my battered heart swells.
I remember the joys, I remember the pain
And I'm loving and living life all over again.

I think of the years all too few—gone too fast.
And accept the stark fact that nothing can last.
So open your eyes Nurse! Open and see,
Not a Crabbit old woman,
Look closer—see me!

The following is, I understand, a nurse's gentle reply to the 'Crabbit' old lady

What do we see, you ask, what do we see?
Yes, we are thinking when seeming to flee.
We may seem to be hard when we hurry and pass,
But there are many of you and too few of us.
We would like more time to sit by you and talk
To bathe you and feed you and help you to walk.
To hear of your lives and things you have done
Your childhood, your husband, your daughter, your son.
But time is against us, there's too much to do,
Patients are many and nurses too few.
We grieve when we see you so sad and alone
With nobody near you, no friends of your own.
We feel all your pain and know your fear
That nobody cares when your end may be near.
But nurses are people with feelings as well
And when we're together, you'll often hear tell
Of the dearest old gran in the very end bed,
And the lovely old dad and the things that he said.
We speak with compassion and love, and feel sad
When we think of your lives and the joy that you've had;
And when the time comes for you to depart,
You leave us behind with an ache in our hearts.
When you come to the long sleep, no more worry and care
There are other old people, and we must be there.
So please understand if we hurry and pass
There are many of you, and too few of us.

My father liked old people and probably carried out more practical acts of kindness for them than his family and friends ever knew.

He would have been able to understand the loneliness of the crabbit old lady and would have sympathized with the nurses. In the QUIET CORNER which follows he tells of patient and nurse who served each other very well.

The Gift of Laughter

QUIET CORNER

BOTH WERE called Mary—but there the similarity ends.

One was at the end of her days, a sweet tired old lady who had long outlived her friends—and the compassion of relatives who might still have visited her. The other was fresh and young, with the gift of laughter that went ringing through the wards where she was a nurse probationer. Her laughter heartened all the patients. In particular it delighted the bedridden old lady to whom 'visiting hour' merely meant the pleasurable wistfulness of watching the callers who passed her bed with slightly detached smiles.

Because the young nurse sensed her loneliness, she would spend odd moments by the old lady's bed, telling her the gossip of the day, showing her snapshots—'That's the one of me taken at Aberdeen. I always spoil them laughing!'

It was the night of the staff dance, and because the old lady's strength was ebbing fast and she was now in the side

ward alone, the little probationer lingered as she went off duty.

'My frock is white net, yards and yards of it. It's got a halter neck and . . . Grandma, would you like to see it?'

So it was that, secretly, against all the rules made for the establishment of order and discipline, the little nurse stole later into the ward and, with dancing eyes and feet, pirouetted in her first party dress before the delighted eyes that misted with sheer delight.

Even as the little nurse was dancing, the old lady passed away to where no one is ever lonely or friendless again.

The end of the story? No, not quite. When they came to gather her few possessions, they found one that was dearest to her beneath her pillow. It was a snapshot—the laughing seaside one that the little probationer had never even missed. The old lady had kept and treasured it. How often must she have looked at the laughing face and derived comfort when loneliness assailed, no one will know.

> *Sweet is the gift of laughter,*
> *A smiling word, and loneliness is gone.*
> *Kindness helps faith. Now and for ever after,*
> *These are the things to build our lives upon.*

November 1953

57

The Way

A TRAVELLER in Malaya was attempting to reach a certain village and by and by he came to the realisation that he was hopelessly lost, with nightfall not far off.

By the greatest good fortune a native came on the scene and agreed to act as his guide for the rest of the way.

Darker and more difficult grew the road, thicker and more tangled the jungle. Still the guide forged ahead, now actually hacking a road through the dense undergrowth. The traveller began to doubt whether his guide really knew where he was going.

'Look here, are you sure you know the way?' he demanded.

His guide turned and looked at him keenly. 'The way?' he said sharply. 'There is no way—I am the way!'

October 1955

. . . the Truth

My father liked a good story like that. He also had a love of poetry. Preachers live in a world where good stories and poems abound. They get changed along the way. One wonders what their original writers, whoever they were, would think of them now!

. . . and the Light

She got in the elevator at the fifteenth floor of the big hotel and the eight of us who were already in shuffled back to make more room.

She was pretty and dressed in black that seemed to add to a touch of grief that lay in her eyes. Along with her, in a little blue coat

'There is not enough darkness in all the world to put out the light of one small candle'

and a cute little face, came a bit of a girl of about four years. We made more room, for little girls who are not very tall must have more room than grown-ups.

And so we stood as the door clanged shut and we started down. Just as we did there came an 'Oh' in a frightened tone from the little girl, and she hid her face in her mother's skirt.

Her mother looked down and said to her—*'You mustn't be frightened. Just open your eyes and look up at the light.'*

And so she did. And all the way down she kept her eyes on the blow-like globe with a clear white light. And reaching the lobby we all of us stood with hat in hand while mother and child went on their way. I don't know, but I imagine that most of us remember the words—YOU MUSTN'T BE FRIGHTENED. JUST OPEN YOUR EYES AND LOOK UP AT THE LIGHT.

A Christmas Carol

QUIET CORNER

THE SCENE is the Children's Ward in a big English hospital. The time—a drab day in November. Why, then, the brightly lit Christmas Tree and the familiar but early strains of a well-loved carol, sung by the nurses and thumped out on the ward piano?

Christmas approaches for the excited youngsters near and dear to us. For one little girl Christmas has already come—and gone. Her name was Kathleen Anne and she was afflicted with a disease for which science has as yet no cure. Christmas was all she could talk of, Christmas and the coming of Santa Claus with the two wishes of her heart, a doll and a pink pram.

Her parents looked distractedly at the tight-lipped specialist, who shook his head emphatically. They would not have Kathleen Anne at Christmas. If she was so set upon a party and on wearing the

59

ballet dress which was waiting for her when she left hospital, they had simply no time to lose.

As you would expect, it was the nurses who saw a way out, and so on an ordinary day in November, after every visitor had gone, to the singing of 'Silent Night' and 'Come all ye faithful', the party got underway. There was a brightly lit tree, surmounted by a fairy in shimmering tiara. There was Santa Claus with a gift for every child, and for Kathleen Anne—believe it or not—a doll and a pink pram! 'Oh, Mummie!' was all she could exclaim, and may we not believe that Heaven's brightest angels looked down in approbation upon all who toiled in off-duty time to make the Christmas dream of one little girl come true.

It is not given to us to understand the inscrutable mystery of the death of a child. But at this season of the birth of a Child, should we not in our prayers remember Kathleen Anne, and should we not see to it that there is not a single little one known to us who does not feel that he or she has a place in this wonderful time when childish dreams and childish hopes really may come true.

December 1954

I find conducting Watchnight Services on Christmas Eve challenging and difficult. They are challenging because there are often many people present who only come on this night. You want the light of the Gospel to be at least *glimpsed* by them on this occasion. And it is always a difficult Service to conduct when you are aware that there are people sitting in the pews who last year sat beside loved ones, now departed.

Mary Mortimer (now Whitehead) is my stepmother. She wrestled with that difficulty in a poem written many years ago. In the intervening years we have both lost loved ones.

'Keeping Christmas is good, but sharing it with others is much better'

Merry Christmas To You!

'A Merry Christmas to you!'
    How often do we greet
Our friends and our relations with
    those words whene'er we meet?
But do we ever pause to think that
    there may be a reason
That for them this Christmas may
    not be a very festive season?

Perhaps they've lost a loved one
    who was very, very dear,
Or they have some secret worry that
    makes the future drear.

Are we wrong, then, thus to greet
    them?
    Why, of course, the answer's 'No!'
They need the cheer of Christmas as
    two thousand years ago.
This world was full of darkness and
    torn with stress and strife,
When suddenly a Child was born
    to bring eternal life.

Man has progressed since early days
    with satellites and such,
But one thing still remains the same
    —we need the Christ-child's touch.

Mary Mortimer

61

Professor Barclay's Christmas Story

AT A Glasgow conference, Ronnie Barclay told me what he regards as the favourite story of his famous father, Professor William Barclay.

In hospital at Christmas-time a little boy learned for the very first time the story of Jesus. He came from a home with no Christian background and he was held in wonder.

The hospital had a sour-faced nurse. The little boy turned to her as she was prodding his bed. 'I never knew about Jesus before. Nurse, have you heard about Jesus?'

Came the clipped reply. 'Of course I have. There's nothing new in that'.

Came the candour of youth. '*You've* heard about Jesus? To look at you, you wouldna' think it!'

December 1975

It is interesting to note that some years after the conference referred to in that QUIET CORNER, Ronnie Barclay and I became colleagues and friends as we worked together for the renewal of the Presbyterian eldership. My father, had he lived long enough, would have been very interested.

I don't remember my father ever talking much about God and Jesus to me as a boy. My father was however insistent upon the value of what he called 'going to Church'.

He was very conscious of his short-comings as a human being. Often when he was angry with someone dear to him, he was really angry with himself for not handling some situation well, for losing his temper or whatever.

I imagine he had trouble looking at his very ordinary short-comings in the light of his Scottish Presbyterian faith. If, however, he were taunted about being a frail Christian, he would reply—'Yes, but I would be a lot less than I am, and a lot worse than I am, without my faith and without my Sunday hour worshipping Almighty God'.

How Christmas
came to 'Roaring Camp'

Roaring Camp was a typical western town in the days of the Gold Rush, with a reputation worse than most. A man's closest friend was a gun and the only meeting place the saloon.

There was only one woman in Roaring Camp. She worked in the saloon. One night in the middle of winter she had a baby. No one knew who the father was and before Lil could say, she died.

The miners were left to look after the baby so they all met in the saloon to decide what they should do.

From somewhere they unearthed an old soap box, though how it came to be there no one knew. None of them had used soap in a long time! They used the box for a cradle. They wrapped some old rags round the baby for clothes, and they put the box in the middle of the saloon floor.

They felt this was all wrong so they sent Jake to the next town with his dog sleigh to buy suitable clothes. When he came back, they put them on the baby. But the clothes made the box all wrong. Jake was told to hitch up his dogs and go back for the best cradle gold could buy.

When he came back, the baby in the new clothes was put in the cradle in the middle of the floor.

For the first time they noticed the dirt on the floor. The floor was scrubbed. This showed up the dirt on the walls and the windows broken by bullets. These had to be repaired.

Because of the baby the whole town had to change. It showed up what they had not seen before.

It did not stop there either. The miners found that they could not touch the baby when their hands were filthy, so they began to wash. They found their unshaven faces frightened the baby so they began to shave.

Because of the baby their appearance had to change. But the biggest change was in their behaviour. Because of the baby, the miners had to change the very way they acted towards each other. The first time there was an argument after the arrival of the baby, the noise of the guns awoke him. They had to stop using their guns. They had even to drop their voices in case they wakened the baby. Roaring Camp had ceased to roar!

Adapted from Bret Harte

63

The following extract is taken from a book entitled *The Valley of the Shadow* by a Lutheran Minister called Hans Lilze – a man who opposed Hitler before and during the war. On Christmas Eve, 1944, while himself a prisoner, he was asked to conduct a Communion Service for another prisoner, Count X. His Christmas congregation consisted of the Count, the Commandant and a violinist who was

Christmas—In Gestapo Cell

' . . . . At the Commandant's suggestion the violinist played a Christmas chorale, exquisitely; then, in this cell, and before this congregation, I read the Gospel for Christmas Day: "Now it came to pass in those days there went out a decree . . .". The violinist played another Christmas chorale; in the meantime I had been able to arrange my thoughts a little about the passage in Isaiah which had filled my mind when I was summoned downstairs. I said to my fellow-prisoners:

'"This evening we are a congregation, part of the Church of Christ, and this great word of divine promise is as true for us today as it was for those of a year ago, among whom, at that time, was your own brother—and for all who this year receive it in faith. Our

chief concern, now," I said, "is to receive this promise in firm faith, and to believe that God, through Jesus Christ, has allowed the eternal light to arise and shine upon this world which is plunged in the darkness of death, and that He will also make this Light to shine for us. At this moment, in our cells, we have practically nothing that makes the Christmas festival so familiar and so lovely, but there is one thing left to us: God's great promise. Let us cling to this promise, and to Him, in the midst of the darkness. Here and now, in the midst of the uncertainty of our prison life, in the shadow of death, we will praise Him by a firm and unshaken faith in His Word, which is addressed to us".

'Then, in the midst of the cell, the Count knelt down upon the hard stone floor, and while I prayed aloud the beautiful old prayer of confession from Thomas a Kempis (which he himself had chosen) and then pronounced absolution, the tears were running down his cheeks. It was a very quiet celebration of the Sacrament full of deep confidence in God; almost palpably the wings of the Divine Mercy hovered over us, as we knelt at the altar in a prison cell on Christmas Eve.

'*We were prisoners, in the power of the Gestapo—in Berlin. But the peace of God enfolded us: it was real and present, "like a Hand laid gently upon us . . . . "*

' Since the Commandant had obviously done all this without permission, and on his own personal responsibility, he could not allow any further conversation. The violinist played a closing chorale; I parted from my fellow-prisoner with a warm handshake, saying: "God bless you, brother X". When we reached the corridor the Commandant shook my hand twice, with an iron grip; he was deeply moved; turning to me, he said: "Thank you! You cannot imagine what you have done for me this evening in my sad and difficult daily work". I was immediately taken back to my cell, but I praised God and indeed, I praised Him from my whole heart that in this building under the shadow of death, and in the face of so much trouble and distress, a Christian congregation had assembled to celebrate Christmas. For it is possible to have every external sign of festivity and comfort and joyful celebrations, and yet not to have a true Christmas congregation, while in the shadow of death and in much trouble of heart, a real Christian congregation can gather at Christmas. It is possible for the candles and the lights to blind our eyes, so that we can no longer see the essential element in Christmas; but the people who "walk in darkness" can perhaps see it better than all who see only the lights of earth.'

Bonhoeffer wrote from his Gestapo cell: 'To be a Christian does not mean to be religious in a particular way . . . but to be a man—not a type of man, but *the man that Christ creates in us.*'

The true dimension of human-ness is not what we are when left to ourselves, but what we have it in us to become when taken out of ourselves into the full potential stature of humanity in Christ.

John Robinson has said: 'How to be human now: that is the greatest single search that unites our distracted world. If the Christian message is to have any relevance, it will be because it comes to men as an answer to that question.'

UNTO US IS BORN A SAVIOUR!

As I have already explained, the Second World War cost my father dearly—not in physical injury as to so many other people, but in terms of his life's direction. He always remained suspicious of the twentieth century German people.

I liked when he was in the congregation at St Ninian's, Bellfield for the Watchnight Service. Often we would ponder readings like those above. I wonder what he would feel now about the reunification of Germany. It is something I do not fear, but then I have not had to experience what my father experienced in this connection.

The Keeper of the Inn

QUIET CORNER

THIS POEM has such moving pathos that I make no apology for printing it after our Christmas issue. Since it arrived anonymously through the Minister's letter-box, I am unable to give the name of the author.

'Oh, if only I had known!'
Said the Keeper of the Inn.
'But to me no hint was shown,
And—I did not let them in!

'Yes, a Star gleamed overhead,
But I could not read the skies,
And I'd given every bed
To the really rich and wise.
And she was so poorly clad,
And he had not much to say,
But—no room for them I had,
So I ordered them away.

'She seemed tired, and it was late
And they begged so hard, that I,
Feeling sorry for her state,
In the stable let them lie.
Had I turned some rich man out,
Just to make a place for them,
I should have killed, beyond a doubt,
All my trade in Bethlehem.

'Then there came the Wise Men three
To the stable, in the morn,
Who announced they'd come to see
The mighty King who had been born.

'And they brought Him gifts of myrrh,
Costly frankincense and gold,
And a great light shone on her,
In that stable, bleak and cold.

'All my patrons now are dead
And forgotten, but today
All the world to peace is led,
By the One I sent away!

'It was my unlucky fate
To be born that Inn to own.
Against the Christ I shut my gate.
Oh—if only I had known!'

Anon

That poem (with a correction about the wise men coming to the stable) was used in many of our Christmas Services at St Ninian's, Bellfield. Later I lost the words. I was re-united with them in 1990 in one of my father's QUIET CORNERS while compiling this book.

'The crib in Woolworth's window captures the true symbol of Christmas. As at Bethlehem, so in Woolworth's window, the Saviour lies amid the tinsel, the commercialism, the dirt, the sin, the laughter and the indifference of the milling crowd.'

Mervyn Stockwood

Superman

Ancient Rome decided to stage a magnificent procession. The finest built, most handsome young man in the city was chosen and covered with gold leaf. He was chosen to be a superman! He was to be, not flesh and blood, but shining and radiant gold. Such was their idea of glory for this great celebration.

As they processed around the streets, before the day was over, the young man was dead. Human bodies aren't made to be covered with gold leaf. The pores of the skin cannot breathe. They can't function when they are overlaid with gold plate. And so the golden man, the superman, was dead before the procession ended.

Could it be that many of us do that to Jesus—either out of a mistaken sense of reverence or because we find him less disturbing that way—covered with tinsel?

The Last Word!

THERE IS one job which I do supremely well. I shall not listen to a word of contradiction. For one hour in the whole year I am perfect, unassailable. The radiant faces of dozens of kiddies at Beechwood Day Nursery assure me that this is so.

To achieve such perfection, of course, I have to lay aside my own indifferent personality and in scarlet and ermine with snowy beard I am annually the breathtaking, captivating figure of childhood— Santa Claus!

Inevitably, after games and singing you sit down for a breather and this is the opportunity for the really curious ones, grappling for the first time with metaphysics and seeking to align the abstract, the mystic, wonderful, with the form possessing definitely some human characteristics.

'Are your whiskers real?' was a question I used to dread because the ignominy of cotton wool whiskers coming adrift in a chubby palm was too awful to contemplate. This year, however, I was well prepared, with magnificent beard and whiskers securely anchored behind the ears. I could with impunity say, 'Real? Of course they're real. Pull 'em gently and see!'

Last year I was profoundly moved when a little girl, caught touching the hem of my garment, stood wide-eyed, trembling, offering the excuse—'I only wanted to touch Santa Claus!' There was nothing just like that on this occasion, but to one charming little girl I clearly lived up to all that the story-books say. Engagingly she chattered about herself, her hair, her pretty dress. Something else was needed, to make me realise that to her I represented all the wonder in creation. Some final phrase was called for.

'Santa Claus . . . ,' she breathed ecstatically. 'I've got on new pants!'

January 1956

By all accounts he was a 'pure dead brilliant' Santa Claus. He did not have to lay aside 'an indifferent personality'. He could enter into the world of children. Perhaps to begin with, however, the disguise did help him.

Later there were to be in his life two children into whose lives he could totally enter, requiring no disguise. These were my children, his grandchildren. He loved to play with them and make toys for them.

He died in 1979 when Debbie was 12 and Stewart Andrew 8. Stewart and I often talk about our own father and son relationship in the light of the one I had with my father. Debbie, now a married woman, talks about him often. She will live all her life with her 'Papa' in her heart. Like me she will, I think, die looking forward to meeting him again.

Who Touched Me?

QUIET CORNER

EVERY YEAR I play Father Christmas at one of the Corporation nurseries, where kiddies are in safe and expert hands all day whilst their mothers lend a hand to industry. Although the lights of Christmas have flickered and gone out—and with them, much of the extra warm-heartedness which lasts, too, for so short a season—I feel you may like to hear one final Christmas story.

I had distributed the gifts and, safely esconced behind a wealth of cotton wool whiskers, was watching the happy youngsters gloating over their new possessions, when, suddenly, at my voluminous sleeve I felt a small but quite perceptible tug.

'Who is it?' I asked and, turning round, I saw a tiny girl in a pink party dress, just managing to hold her own with a tremulous smile before the no doubt awe-inspiring figure of Santa.

'Hello, my dear, what can I do for you?' I asked, as reassuringly as I could.

Emotions chased themselves across her face. One of them at least told her to run, but the tremulous smile and the brave little maid both held their ground. Her hand was now actually in mine.

'Please—,' she said. 'I just wanted to touch Santa Claus!'

70

I was tremendously moved. I had got there with some difficulty and was already calculating what I might be able to do in the business sphere with what was left of the afternoon. Mundane things were at the back of my mind, yet to one little girl I represented —most unworthily—all the wonder and the mystery in the world!

'Who touched me?' said Christ to the woman in the crowd who touched Him for much the same reason. Alas, the difference is that I was merely a fake, as that little girl will learn in days to come.

January 1955

The Two Dolls' Houses

QUIET CORNER

IN MY day I have made two dolls' houses. Perhaps you would like to hear about them. One is a happy story, the other not happy at all, since it is a sad reflection upon the sorry times in which we live.

The first doll's house was made for Eileen, who is my youngest friend. She is a lovely child, an entrancing mite with loving ways and a built-in sense of diplomacy which, in a three-year old, is

71

nothing less than remarkable. When she joined our Primary Sunday School she could not be seen over the top of the pews, a situation which she is rapidly seeking to correct. As an honorary uncle, I claimed the honour of making her doll's house a long time ago. It was a privilege in more ways than one, because I felt I was standing in, as it were, for the young father who would have made that doll's house and much besides, if he had not lost his life with reckless gallantry in seeking to save the life of a friend.

So Eileen had her doll's house on Christmas Day, and what a miracle it is that can take some spars of wood, some paper, paint, some glue and wire and transform them into twin stars of delight in the eyes of a much-loved little girl!

The other story, I have warned you, has no such happy ending. The other doll's house was made much earlier for the Corporation children's nursery, where I have the privilege each year to play Santa Claus. Intended for daily use by dozens of children of all kinds, it was designed for strength and sturdiness. Strong and sturdy it certainly was, but alas, not strong or sturdy enough to survive the attacks of youthful vandals who regularly subject this nursery to their un-welcome attentions, presumably looking for the sweets and small comforts devised by a devoted Matron and her staff for the benefit of their tiny tots. The treasured doll's house was smashed beyond repair by someone who was clearly determined that it would never function again. The children are not entirely without a doll's house I am glad to note. They now have a small tin contraption, useful, but unlikely to arouse dark destructive tendencies in the mind of someone to whom even the possessions of little helpless children are in no wise sacred.

January 1963

He was to make, in due course, a third dolls' house—one for his grand-daughter, as indeed he made a toy railway for his grandson. Debbie's dolls' house was magnificent—two storeyed, lit, furnished with every detail. I have yet to be forgiven by Debbie and her mother for one day, when Debbie was a teenager, giving the dolls' house to one of Stewart Andrews' friends for his little sister. I had not appreciated the value of the making of the house. Perhaps, one day, my son will restore to his sister a dolls' house of his own making.

The Psalm and the Shepherd

THIS WONDERFUL little story was told by Revd J B Coupar when he recently exchanged pulpits with our own minister.

At a dinner held by a number of business men there were guests from a great variety of professions and it was decided that during the evening each guest, in turn, should entertain the company. At last it was the turn of a well-known actor, who held his audience spell-bound with the quality of his rendering of the Twenty-third Psalm.

Triumphantly he resumed his place, and now there was only one man left to speak, the uninspiring figure of a little old clergyman, who confessed he was somewhat nonplussed, for it had been his own intention to repeat the Twenty-third Psalm.

'Go on, go on,' said the well-known actor. 'I've no doubt your rendering will be different from mine!' He smiled a little to himself.

Slowly at first, falteringly, his voice rising in strength, the old man repeated the grand, stirring, heart-warming words of the noblest of psalms.

In utter silence the audience heard him, and as he concluded there was a perfect storm of applause. The actor himself was on his feet to grasp the old man's hand.

'Ah, sir,' he said, with emotion. 'I know the Psalm. But you—you know the Shepherd!'

May 1958

73

Script or Story?

Think about an actor—locked within the lines of his script. Someone in the past has written the words, devised the scenes, programmed the emotions and the flow of the drama. Day after day the actor goes on stage performing these lines again and again. Sometimes we feel like that—scripted, to some extent programmed—getting involved in the same scenes, even though the cast of players around us may change.

There are three common and quite easily recognisable roles:

Persecutor   continually running down a person, an institution
or whatever; highly critical beyond what
could be described as constructive.

Rescuer   continually helping people who don't need help,
smothering; doing for people who don't need
being done for, doing for instead of enabling
people to choose and do for themselves.

Victim   continually claiming to be incapable, inadequate,
beyond hope; seeking advice and help with no
intention of taking either, if it involves action and
change.

We can spend a lot of time and energy acting out these roles or jumping from one to another. Most probably these roles were learned, and our 'favourite one' chosen—quite unconsciously—when we were little people in the land of the grown ups, who exercised so much power over us. Often we act out a role with no awareness that we are doing it. If we have been well-programmed, perhaps all is well. Often things are not so because we are all children of imperfect parents. Living our today controlled by our yesterday can be destructive of our tomorrow.

On page after page of the New Testament we see Jesus *enable* people, give them the opportunity, to escape physical and psychological SCRIPTS. He doesn't persecute people. Nor does he rescue them. He provides opportunities for people to stand up on their own feet and begin to live with a new creativity if they want to. He calls us to live with the creativity of that old minister who knew not just the psalm, but the shepherd who calls us to write the STORY of our life and to develop the potential within us.

◊

The Little Chap who ran to Church

THE LOVELIEST day of this grudging summer was for me one of the saddest and most perplexing days of my life. On it I stood by the grave of the tiny son of a dear friend and watched strong men weep as the coffin of the little boy who lost his life in a motor accident was lowered to the earth.

The little cemetery at Newburgh stands on a slope between Clatchard Craig, eastmost spur of the Ochils, and the quiet upper reaches of the Tay. We listened there to strong, reassuring words, while on the upper slopes a diesel engine pulled its clanking load, and overhead a thrush sang heedlessly from an azure sky.

Too often I have stood by the graves of young people and always, I confess it, I am assailed with doubt. That such things happen; is it the care—or the carelessness—of God? Only five, he was so young to die. With tears in her eyes a neighbour told me how often she had watched the little chap scamper ahead of his parents on their way to church. Their faith, I then realised, must be even more shaken than my own.

The care—or the carelessness—of God? Not for one moment will I believe that God really wanted a little fellow, just back from joyous holiday, to perish in the car of the aunt who loved him. But this material world revolves by natural laws and I believe that God, Who tenderly notes each sparrow as it falls, cannot, by the very laws He created, be expected to suddenly reverse them, even to save a precious young life. At the best we have here no abiding city. Andrew has no need of our pity, but spare a thought in your prayers for a mother in her bewildering grief, for an aunt denied even the joy that her own two bairns escaped. For the father I am less anxious. He is much concerned with the welfare of youth both physically and spiritually. In this I am sure he will redouble his efforts and in years to come many a lad benefiting from his wise counsel will never realise how much he owes to the little chap who ran to church, whose body lies beneath Clatchard Craig, whose soul is serene, shining, safe for ever in a Heavenly Father's care.

They asked him—Is it well with the child?
He answered—It is well.

September 1963

A Quiet Lady Passes

QUIET CORNER

QUITE A few in St Andrew's Church and many in the ranks of the old age pensioners of Dundee, will mourn the passing of our former member, Mrs Jenny Butchart, late of 7 Dalrymple Street, and latterly of Fortrose.

When she was with us, she delivered *The Wyvern* in fair weather and foul, although in latter years the winter weather was her unrelenting foe. Day in and day out, too, she served the old age pensioners, many of whom must have been infinitely hardier than herself. Truly she served beyond her strength.

To me she was among the loveliest of women. In an age which foolishly assesses worth by mod cons and status symbols, Jenny Butchart was a lady in her own right. Gracious, kindly, wise in counsel, she had known royalty both at home and abroad—but you would never have learned it from her. Although with the death of her husband, some of whose lovely poems we have published in *The Wyvern*, much of the brightness of life had departed, she lived on for her social work, for her daughter, her grandson and tiny granddaughter, who were the joy of her existence.

At the service at Dundee Crematorium, I was frankly incapable of the usual amount of sorrow on such occasions. Winter winds were normally so cruel to her. Somewhere on that cold, winter day, somewhere 'where falls not hail nor rain, nor any snow, nor ever wind blows loudly?', I felt her still, a vital, smiling presence, with her beloved husband, hand-in-hand. That was her own quiet, unshakable conviction. I believe that this is so.

'In my Father's house are many mansions. If it were not so, I would have told you.'

September 1962

> ## Death Came
> ## the Other Night
>
> I dreamt Death came the other
> night,
> Heaven's gracious gates swung
> wide.
> With kindly grace an Angel bright
> Ushered me inside.
> And there, to my astonishment
> Stood folk I'd known on earth,
> Some I'd harshly judged and
> deemed
> 'Unfit', or 'little worth'.
> Indignant words rose to my lips,
> But never were set free,
> For every face showed stunned
> surprise
> NO ONE EXPECTED ME!
>
> *Anon*

Many a QUIET CORNER focussed on the harsh reality of life's unfairness and the fact of our mortality. The one on the next page was written when my father had the likelihood of his own imminent mortality on his mind. He returns to his 'stand up for Jesus' theme. Jesus died able to hold together the harsh reality of life's suffering and unfairness and the reality of the love of God. What else is there to offer and to stand up for?

Stand Up! Stand Up for Jesus!

WHEN I take Morning Service at Murthly Parish Church, then the even more beautiful Caputh Parish Church for Revd F Routledge Bell, I hold later a service for the patients and available staff of Murthly Hospital. At the Hospital, the above hymn is an outstanding favourite and I think they would sing it as lustily every week.

Its author, Dr George Duffield, was born at Carlisle, Pennsylvania, in 1818, and followed his father into the ministry of the Presbyterian Church of America.

The hymn was inspired by a sad incident. His friend Revd Dudley Tyng, a most eloquent preacher, was caught in a corn-threshing machine and his arm severed from his body. Before he died that day he sent a farewell message to those who would gather together that evening for prayer, telling them to 'stand up for Jesus'.

On the following Sunday, Dr Duffield preached a funeral sermon and read out the verses he had written in honour of his friend. The verse below refers specifically to the loss of Dudley Tyng and is not included in our hymn books.

'Stand up! Stand up for Jesus!
Each soldier to his post.
Close up the broken column
And shout through all the host.
Make good the loss so heavy,
In those that still remain,
And prove to all around you
That death itself is gain.'

January 1979

'How does the prophet know that God will neither leave us nor forsake us?
How does the psalmist know that the broken-hearted and the afflicted will be comforted?

'Because they themselves had dark days and lonely nights.
That's why!
Because they themselves had gone through it.

'These Scripture truths are fragrant flowers that their own fingers plucked from the gardens of human experience.
Sometimes the thorns pricked them, but they held on to the flowers.

' "I will not leave you comfortless," Christ says.
And only those whose hearts have been left desolate . . .
      only those who have needed comforting . . .
         needed it desperately . . .
know how true that promise is.

'Christ does not leave us comfortless, but we have to be in dire need of comfort to know the truth of His promise.

'It is in times of calamity . . .
     in days and nights of sorrow and trouble
       that the presence
         the sufficiency
           and the sympathy of God grow very sure and
             very wonderful.

'Then we find out that the grace of God is sufficient for all our needs
     for every problem
     and for every difficulty
for every broken heart, and for every human sorrow'.

Peter Marshall

The Problem of Falling Rocks

Often at funeral services I read the words on the previous page. They come from one of the sermons of a man called Peter Marshall.

Peter Marshall was a Scots boy who went to America. He became a minister, a very famous minister, who in due course became chaplain to the American Senate.

The words come from a sermon he called—'The Problem of Falling Rocks', by which he meant the awesome, shattering things which can suddenly drop upon us out of an otherwise clear blue sky.

Peter Marshall, Dorothy and Gordon, mentioned earlier, and the little chap who ran to church, all died before their time. For old Jim, below, it was different . . . .

The Quiet Faith of Old Jim

QUIET CORNER

HOGMANY 1978, in a city hospital. From the next bed came the voice of old Jim, aged 78, whose life had been one of incredible hardship. Said he: 'You read the Bible. There's one bit I've never understood. Would you explain it to me?' 'If I can, Jim'.

'In my Father's house are many mansions. What does that mean, and how does it end?'

'It means, Jim, Jesus was trying to explain as simply as he could that our Heavenly Father's home has countless dwelling-places—mansions is an out-of-date word. The dwelling-places are for simple-hearted believers and it seems reasonable to suppose that there we will be re-united with those we have loved and lost here'.

Jim seemed astounded. 'Special dwelling-places, and I might have one and not have to trauchle up 63 steps . . . .'

'Truly, Jim, I would say you have more than a chance, and you can forget all about those 63 steps.'

'And the passage, how does it end?'

'It's beginning, John 14, is even more important. "You believe in

God; believe also in me". At the end Jesus simply says, "If it were not so, I would have told you".'

'If it were not so, I would have told you,' Jim whispered. 'All we have to do is believe what he says . . . . '

There was silence in the bay. In distant bays the welcome to the New Year grew slightly in volume. From the next bed came the sound of quiet breathing. Old Jim was sleeping the sleep of utter contentment.

February 1979

I think it was my father who was Jim's fellow patient and spiritual guide. My father, though not much of a smoker, died of lung cancer. I think he probably had a hard time as his terminal situation became apparent to him. I don't think my mother understood much about such a situation and at the time I was not skilled in these things and so of less help to him than later I might have been.

He probably bargained with God for more time. The time he wanted was to be able to look after his wife whom he had made so dependent upon him. He had tried so hard to make up to her in time and attention what he had not been able to give her in material possessions.

One day when he was supposed to be at home—he was, as it turned out, dying—he got out of his bed, put his coat on over his pyjamas, got out the car and drove to my mother's doctor's surgery to save her the difficulty of coming home on public transport.

In his last months happily he and I got on well and communicated better than we had ever done before. Somehow we had always been competitors. He had been determined that I should get a better break in life than he had got—and yet he always seemed to be struggling to keep up with me, for he had left home and school at 14 years old. I remember him proudly getting his Higher English during the time I worked in Kilmarnock. Needless to say he got an 'A' band.

He became a Reader and so licensed by The Church of Scotland to conduct worship. Some of his proudest moments thereafter were when he was allowed to occupy his son's pulpit in Kilmarnock. Mind you, I had to read about this in something he wrote in *The Wyvern*! The St Ninian's people loved him. I had to remind him that the real test is standing in the same pulpit, Sunday after Sunday, year in and year out. However, I did not need to make any reference to ha'penny biscuits! The back row could hear every word. The congregation loved the older version and I was pleased for them and for him.

He came to terms with his impending death though he didn't speak about it directly to me. One day, as I sat at the foot of his bed—the bed and the bedroom which years earlier had been mine—he said, 'Tell your people (by which he meant the Bellfield congregation) that what you tell them about is true'. I took this to mean that at the end of his anything but tranquil life, he had found the peace of God.

His spiritual life had begun when he had gone with a group of boys to scoff at a street evangelist. He had, he told me, started to scoff but had stopped to listen, long after his pals had moved on. From that day he had tried to be God's person and happily left this life, full of flaws, but nonetheless God's person.

When it becomes my turn to leave this life, I hope I shall do so as well as my father did. I hope I shall do so as God's person. When the time comes, I look forward to meeting him again. We have much to talk about; so much to get right about each other; so much to understand that was not understood; so many 'sorries' to say. By then, of course, sorries will not be required. Hugs will suffice.

Why God Made Hugs

Everyone was meant to share
God's all-abiding love and care;
He saw that we would need to know
A way to let these feelings show.

So God made hugs—a special sign,
And symbol of his love divine,
A circle of our open arms
To hold in love and keep out harm.

One simple hug can do its part
To warm and cheer another's heart.
A hug's a bit of heaven above
That signifies his perfect love.

Jill Wolfe

ACKNOWLEDGMENTS

While every effort has been made to trace the holders of copyright on all non-original material contained within this book, due to the nature of the sources this has not always proved possible. The Publisher would appreciate any relevant information in order that sources may be acknowledged accurately in any subsequent editions.

Acknowledgment and thanks are due for the following :

'I said a prayer for you today . . .' (p1); *'The little toy dog . . .'*, Eugene Field (5); *Don't Quit* (17); *Tame Ducks* (18); *Children Learn What They Live* (24); *Life's Lessons* (26); *'Is it any wonder . . .?'*, H G Wells (29); *All In The April Evening*, a hymn by Hugh S Robertson (31); *The Great Renewal*, Cardinal Cushing (35); *Some Be-Attitudes* (48-49); *Footprints* (51); *'Blessed are they . . .'*, Mrs Janet Logie (53); *'What do you see nurses . . . ?'* (54); *'What do we see, you ask . . . ?'* (55); *. . . And The Light* (58); *Merry Christmas To You!*, Mary Mortimer (61); *How Christmas came to 'Roaring Camp'*, adapted from Bret Harte (63); *Christmas—In Gestapo Cell*, from *The Valley of the Shadow*, Hans Lilze, translated by Olive Wyon, SCM Press Ltd, London, 1950 (64-65); *'Oh if only I had known . . . !'* (66); *'The crib in Woolworth's . . .'*, Mervyn Stockwood (68); *Death Came the Other Night* (77); *'How does the prophet know . . . ?'*, from a sermon by Peter Marshall, from *Mister Jones, Meet the Master*, Collins Fount, London, 1954 (79); *Why God Made Hugs*, Jill Wolfe (82)